Design, Analysis, and Optimization of Supply Chains

Design, Analysis, and Optimization of Supply Chains

A *System Dynamics Approach*

William R. Killingsworth

Design, Analysis, and Optimization of Supply Chains: A System Dynamics Approach
Copyright © Business Expert Press, LLC, 2011.

First published in 2011 by
Business Expert Press, LLC
222 East 46th Street, New York, NY 10017
www.businessexpertpress.com

ISBN-13: 978-1-60649-251-2 (paperback)

ISBN-13: 978-1-60649-252-9 (e-book)

DOI: 10.4128/9781606492529

A publication in the Business Expert Press Supply and Operations Management collection

Collection ISSN: 2156-8189 (print)
Collection ISSN: 2156-8200 (electronic)

Cover design by Jonathan Pennell
Interior design by Scribe Inc.

First edition: May 2011

10 9 8 7 6 5 4 3 2 1

Printed in the United States of America.

To my parents, Bob and Frances Killingsworth,
and my children, Sarah and Will

Abstract

Almost everything made today is manufactured by large networks of companies. Hundreds, if not thousands, of companies provide components, subassemblies, and major assemblies to a final manufacturer or integrator. These large distributed supply chains have created many problems and headaches across a variety of industries. At supply chain forums, it is not unusual to hear grumblings such as the following:

- I've got very unhappy customers and lost sales due to inventory shortages.
- Supplier problems are causing a late introduction of my new product.
- Large inventories, obsolete products, and write-offs are killing my financials.
- A key supplier went out of business and I just now found out, what do I do?
- We seem to lurch from one supply chain problem to another, never finding a stable ground.
- How do you manage something that is so complex?

Today's supply chains are not only highly complex in terms of the number of companies involved but also dynamically complex in that their behavior and performance variations over time range from "hard to comprehend" to baffling. No wonder management is so difficult and challenging. Developing an intuitive grasp of supply chain dynamic behavior is the first step in driving performance improvement.

In this book, a system dynamics framework for analyzing complex supply chain performance is presented. The feedback nature of supply chains is demonstrated and dynamic simulation models are used to examine the counterintuitive behavior that arises from time delays, lack of information, and incorrect planning assumptions. The benefits of establishing push–pull boundaries in supply chains are shown to provide increased customer service levels with modest, if not reduced, levels of inventory. Dynamic supply chain models are used to determine product lifecycle costs and the impacts of improved reliability on lifecycle costs. A basic system dynamics model is used to show that the goal of a "lean and mean" supply chain can be dangerous in periods of economic, political, and climatic volatility, and strategies are developed for improved supply chain management and performance.

Supply chain executives are faced increasingly with greater complexity, faster velocities, heightened volatility, and demands for cost reduction. This is an incendiary mix of business conditions. A dynamic perspective and system dynamics models as presented in this book can provide the tools for facing these challenging demands.

Keywords

Supply chain, system dynamics, dynamic modeling, simulation, push-pull boundary, inventory, reliability, volatility, lifecycle costs

Contents

Acknowledgments

Many friends and colleagues have been highly supportive in the development of this book. First, I want to thank the great people at Business Expert Press: David Parker, Scott Isenberg, and Cindy Durand; and at Scribe, Bill Klump. Working with them has been a pleasure. I want to thank MIT Professor David Simchi-Levi and the members of the MIT Forum for Supply Chain Innovation. Their encouragement, guidance, and advice have been invaluable. I also want to thank my research sponsors at the U.S. Army Aviation and Missile Command: Ronnie Chronister, Bill Andrews, Artro Whitman, Brian Wood, Johnnie Bradt, Wayne Bruno, and Josh Kennedy. At NASA, John Vickers and Mike Galluzzi have been instrumental in support of the research and modeling activities. Neil Orringer, Eugene Gholz, and Steve Linder at OSD have taken an active lead in supply chain studies, and I am grateful for their support. I must also thank my friends and colleagues at the University of Alabama in Huntsville: Dr. Richard Rhoades, Dr. Kenneth Sullivan, Chris Sauter, Nelson Martin, Joe Paxton, Brian Tucker, Teri Martin, and Karen Hancock. Without their support, this book would not have been possible. Dr. Richard Amos, CEO of Colsa Corporation, has been a friend and a supporter of innovative supply chain analysis. Bruce Kaplan at LMI has supported analytical research on supply chains and provided research opportunities. Robert Glitz at AAR Corporation has long recognized the benefits of system dynamics, and I greatly appreciate the opportunity of working with him. I also want to acknowledge the interest and support of the System Dynamics Society and its Executive Director, Roberta Spencer. Dan Tripp, Dr. Simone Caruthers, and Jennifer Webster have provided valuable friendship and support over many years. Finally, I want to thank Dee, PoohBear, and Razzy for their unfailing support and love.

Introduction

Reading the *Wall Street Journal* in January of 2010, I did a double take when I saw the title of a front-page article: "'Bullwhip' Hits Firms as Growth Snaps Back."[1] The title seemed truly unbelievable. The article recounted how Caterpillar had recently told its steel suppliers that it would more than double its purchases of the metal in the coming year—even if Caterpillar's own sales stayed flat. The *Journal* rhetorically asked, "How is that possible?" and then gave the answer as, "Chalk it up to the 'bullwhip effect,' which is reverberating across the U.S. economy." Wait a minute! The bullwhip is "reverberating across the U.S. economy"? I thought the bullwhip problem had been solved by Massachusetts Institute of Technology (MIT) professor Jay Forrester in 1958 and then again in 1997 by Stanford professor Hau Lee. I was obviously very much mistaken. The bullwhip effect had not been solved, and the dynamic behavior of supply chains was still very much misunderstood and the source of problems for thousands of companies.

What is the bullwhip effect? As defined in the *Wall Street Journal* article, the phenomenon is called the "bullwhip because even small increases in demand can cause a big snap in the need for parts and materials further down the supply chain." The effect was first described by Jay Forrester of the MIT Sloan School of Management in a groundbreaking article in the *Harvard Business Review* of July/August 1958. In that article, "Industrial Dynamics—a Major Breakthrough for Decision Makers," Forrester analyzed a very simple supply chain with only three stages or tiers: a retailer, a distributor, and a production factory in a hard-goods industry such as household appliances. Using a simulation model, he demonstrated how a small variation in customer orders at the retail level led, over time, to big swings in production and inventory for the manufacturer. But on an even more basic level, Forrester demonstrated the dynamic behavior of the system and how supply chain management was representative of feedback control and that decisions, delays, and predictions (i.e., forecasts) could produce either good control or highly unstable behavior.

Forrester had several fundamental insights:

1. The overall system, from raw materials to final sales, was actually composed of multiple subsystems: production, distribution, and retail.
2. Management was conducted at the subsystem level, and decisions and actions made at the subsystem or local level were not necessarily the best for the overall system.
3. Management decisions were oriented to achieve desired local results, and variables such as average sales, current inventory, and estimated lead times were used to reach a decision on matters such as the ordering rate to suppliers; in this fashion, each management subsystem was very much a feedback-control system.
4. Lack of information sharing and delays in the system were major features of the system structure and contributed greatly to overall system behavior and performance.

In his model, Forrester identified three principal types of orders used to manage the subsystems: orders that directly reflect sales; orders to adjust inventories in response to changing levels of business volume; and orders to fill the supply lines with in-process orders and shipments. These ordering components operated at each level: factory, distributor, and retailer. Forrester treated these orders in the following fashions:

1. After a sales analysis and purchasing delay (3, 2, and 1 weeks, respectively, for the three levels of retail, distribution, and production), orders to the next higher level of the system are based on the actual sales made by the ordering level.
2. After a time for averaging out sales fluctuations (8 weeks), a gradual upward or downward adjustment is made in inventories as the rate of sales increases or decreases. This is a corrective feedback action taken to move inventories toward a desired level.
3. The orders in process (i.e., orders in the mail, unfilled orders at the supplier, and goods in transit) are proportional to the level of business activity and to the length of time required to fill an order. Both increased sales volume and increased delivery lead time necessarily result in increased total orders in the supply pipeline.

Forrester assumed that, as in most real-life businesses, the ordering rate was based on some presumption about future sales. For his model, he used the conservative practice of basing the ordering rate on the assumption that sales are most likely to continue at or near their present level—in essence, a rolling average over time. Forrester developed a set of equations that described mathematically the ordering processes and how the resultant shipments changed inventory levels and the availability of product. He could then simulate the behavior of the system over time and demonstrate how the overall system responded to changes in customer sales.

In the simulation, Forrester assumed a 10% increase in retail customer orders occurred in January. Because of accounting, purchasing, and mailing delays, the increase in orders to the distributor from the retailer did not reach the 10% level until a month later. However, the rise did not stop at 10%, but actually reached a peak of 16% in March because the retailer made additional orders to (a) increase inventories somewhat and (b) raise the level of orders and goods in transit in the supply chain by 10% to correspond to the 10% increase in sales. Forrester noted that the inventory and pipeline order increments were nonrepeating, or transient, additions to the order rate, and when the associated targets had been met, the retailer's order to the distributors dropped back to the basic and continuing 10% increase.

The incoming orders at the distributor were well above retail sales for several months, reaching a 16% increase. Since the distributor did not know actual sales to the final consumer, these incoming orders were interpreted by the distributor as true increases in business volume of the same amount. The distributor's orders to the factory, therefore, included not only the 16% increase in orders they themselves received but also a corresponding increase for distributor inventories and for orders and goods in transit between distributor and factory. As a result, orders to the factory warehouse reached a peak of 28% above the previous levels. One must now ask, what are the implications for manufacturing orders? Production orders at the factory were placed on the basis of the increasing factory warehouse orders and the falling warehouse inventory, which dropped 13% due to the increased shipments arising from higher orders from the distributor. As a result, the factory output, delayed by a factory lead time of 7 weeks, reached a peak in June that was 40% above the December level prior to the increased consumer sales. With retail sales still at 10% above December, the factory increase is four times as great. Bullwhip!

Forrester's model, however, demonstrated that the feedback management and control process did, over time, function in a corrective fashion. As retailers began to satisfy their inventory requirements, they began reducing their order rate. In a similar manner, over time, distributors realized they had built up an order rate, inventory, and a supply-line rate in excess of needs. This excess was then taken out of orders to the factory. In September and October, 9 and 10 months after the increase in customer orders, factory output was 3% below December and 13% below current customer retail sales. Several months later, the system finally reached a steady and appropriate solution to the 10% increase in sales.

Forrester was able to show that, as a result of the industry structure and the typical business inventory and ordering processes, more than a year was required before all ordering and manufacturing rates stabilized at their proper rates corresponding to the retail-sales increase of 10%, an increase that was minor compared to the bullwhip that was initiated and then finally constrained. Forrester went on to investigate the implications of cyclical customer sales, reduced clerical and processing times, and limited factory production capacity. He also demonstrated how improved sales data at the factory could help reduce volatility and the bullwhip effect.

In 1997, nearly 40 years after Forrester's article, Stanford professor Hau Lee published an article in the Spring 1997 *MIT Sloan Management Review* titled "The Bullwhip Effect in Supply Chains." In this article, he described how executives at Procter & Gamble (P&G) had noticed that modest variations in sales of P&G's Pampers brand disposable diapers were accompanied by much more variable orders to P&G from distributors, and that P&G's orders of materials to their suppliers were even greater. As Lee noted, "While the consumers, in this case, the babies, consumed diapers at a steady state, the demand order variabilities in the supply chain were amplified as they moved up the supply chain." Again, the bullwhip effect!

Lee's analysis led to a number of strategies for reducing the bullwhip effect. The results are presented in Figure i.1.

A few of the key stabilizing suggestions made by Lee included the following:

Causes of bullwhip	Demand forecast	Order batching	Price fluctuations	Shortage gaming
• Information Sharing	• Understanding systems dynamics • Use point-of-sale (POS) data • Electronic data interchange (EDI) • Internet • Computer-assisted ordering (CAO)	• EDI • Internet ordering		• Sharing sales capacity and inventory data
• Channel alignment	• Vendor-managed inventory (VMI) • Discount for information sharing • Consumer direct	• Discount for truckload assortment • Delivery appointments • Consolidation • Logistics outsourcing	• Continuous replenishment program (CRP) • Everyday low cost (EDLC)	• Allocation based on past sales
• Operational efficiency	• Lead time reduction • Echelon-based inventory control	• Reduction in fixed cost of ordering by EDI or electronic commerce • CAO	• Everyday low price (EDLP) • Activity-based costing (ABS)	

Figure i.1. Causes of the bullwhip.

1. Everyday low price and everyday low cost. This strategy, so effectively implemented by Walmart, reduces the variations in retail sales and stabilizes the ordering process.

2. Sharing sales, capacity, and inventory data. Again, this strategy has been broadly implemented by Walmart so that shipments more accurately reflect consumer demand.

3. Vendor-managed inventory. This strategy has been implemented in many manufacturing environments in which the inventory of the components and subassemblies arriving at the final factory is replenished and managed by the suppliers, not the factory management. Planned production rates are shared with the suppliers, and the suppliers plan shipments to maintain the incoming parts inventory between minimum and maximum values.

4. Understanding system dynamics. Lee realized that uncertainties in supply and demand would always be present in dealing with management of large-scale supply chains. These uncertainties would initiate, after some time delay, corrective actions in the form of corrective feedback control, and these controls, because of delays and limited information, would create dynamics, not an instantaneous movement to an optimal solution. Without an understanding of the system dynamics, the bullwhip and other undesirable responses would be likely.

Yet, in 2010, 50 years after Forrester and 15 years after Lee, the *Wall Street Journal* reported that the bullwhip effect "is reverberating across the U.S. economy." The message is clear: the dynamics of supply chains and large supply networks are still not well understood and major inefficiencies are the costly result. As supply chains have become more global and increasingly complex, supply chain dynamics and the associated risks and costs plague companies around the world. This book follows the lead of Forrester in using system dynamics to examine these issues and to develop guidelines and solutions for managing increasingly complex and dynamic global operations. Who knows? Perhaps in another 50 years we will be able to grasp dynamic behavior and more effectively manage our global strategic supply chains.

CHAPTER 1

A Static Versus a Dynamic View of Supply Chains

Introduction

Supply chains are often viewed as a simple, static system with constant demand, constant orders, and constant production. Generally, these supply chains are viewed as a simple linear "chain" of participants such as a retail store, a distributor, a factory, and perhaps a key supplier to the factory as shown in Figure 1.1.

At the next level of complexity, these linear chains are viewed as a static stochastic system having constant means and constant standard deviations for demand, orders, and production. This statistically based view of the static supply chain resulted in several well-known optimization solutions such as the *economic order quantity* and *optimum reorder points*.[1] These optimal solutions determine an ordering strategy that minimizes cost for an assumed level of customer service. The well-known equation for the reorder point, as shown here, includes the demand expected over the lead time as the key component and a safety factor that reflects uncertainty in demand and lead time.

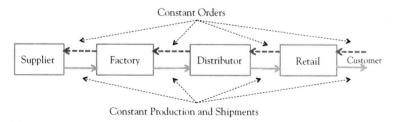

Figure 1.1. A basic review of a static supply chain.

The equation for the optimal reorder point is given by:

Reorder Point = (D)(L) + $z\sqrt{((L)(STD)^2 + (D)^2 (STL)^2)}$

Where

D = Average Demand for the Product

L = Average Lead Time for the Product

z = Service Factor Determined by Fill Rate; for a 90% service level, z=1.29; for a 95% service level, z=1.65; for a 98% service level, z=2.05.

STD = Standard Deviation of Demand

STL = Standard Deviation of Lead Time

The equation for the optimum order quantity is given by:

Order Quantity = $\sqrt{(2KD/h)}$

Where

K = Cost of an Order (set-up costs, shipping, etc.)

D = Average Demand

h = Holding Cost of Inventory (approximated as a percentage carrying cost (25%) times the value of the part).

Thus, once the reorder point is reached, the order quantity is proportional to demand and the cost of an order and is inversely proportional to the holding cost. Thus, if ordering costs are high, then the equation tends to order a higher quantity and reduce the number of orders. On the other hand, if an item is expensive with high holding costs, then the equation tends to order a lower quantity and reduce inventory holding costs. These equations provide useful guidance and insight but, in a dynamic system with time delays and lack of information sharing, they are as likely to create the bullwhip as other ordering processes.

In today's supply chains, complexity arises not only from dynamics but also from the sheer number of participating entities. The typical supply chain involves hundreds, if not thousands, of suppliers, multiple factories, numerous distribution centers, and customers spread across the globe. These supply chains are often depicted as shown in Figure 1.2. Although more complex, they are again primarily analyzed in a static mode of constant flows of orders and material or with constant statistics. These more complex networks can also be analyzed for minimum cost at a specified level of customer service. These optimization solutions, however, fail to predict supply chain dynamics and the substantial swings

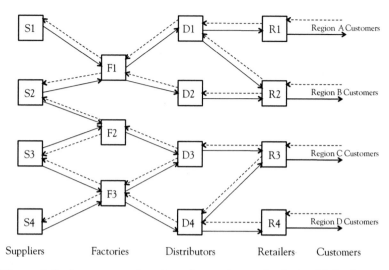

Figure 1.2. A more complex view of a static supply chain. Multiple suppliers supplying multiple factories with multiple distribution centers and multiple regions of customers.

that can occur in inventories, orders, and shipments as in the bullwhip. In order to understand and correct those problems, a dynamic view and model of the supply chain is required.

System Dynamics

System dynamics is a modeling and simulation approach to studying the behavior of complex systems over time. The approach was developed by Jay Forrester at MIT in the mid-1950s and the 1960s. System dynamics focuses on internal feedback loops and the time delays that affect the dynamics of the entire system. Forrester treated a complex system as a system of stocks and flows where the flows, or rates of change, were determined via feedback loops. Forrester's key insight was that changes in stocks (sometimes called *levels*) occur only through associated rates of change, not through a correlation with other variables. A system dynamics model focuses on those key rates that increase or reduce a stock or level over time. For example, a retailer's inventory is reduced by the shipment rate to customers and is increased by shipments received from a distributor. The dynamics of the inventory level are thus the accumulation (or, mathematically, the integration) of all flows into and out of the retailer's inventory. This structure is often shown as pictured in Figure 1.3.

In the simulation of a system dynamics model, given an initial condition for the retail inventory, future inventory levels are developed by mathematically integrating these two flows over a sequence of discrete time steps. Thus the inventory after a small time interval is equal to the initial inventory plus the time step, Δt, multiplied by the shipment rate from distributors during that time interval, minus the time step multiplied by the shipment rate to customers during that time interval:

$$I_1 = I_0 + (\Delta t)(\text{Shipment Rate from Distributors})_{01} - (\Delta t)(\text{Shipment Rate to Customers})_{01}$$

The next calculation for the inventory level is then given as:

$$I_2 = I_1 + (\Delta t)(\text{Shipment Rate from Distributors})_{12} - (\Delta t)(\text{Shipment Rate to Customers})_{12}$$

For the simulation, Δt must be considerably shorter than the time delays within the system, such as shipping times, order processing times, and so forth. Since retailers may not always have adequate inventory for immediate shipment, Forrester's model necessarily included a level for unfilled orders. This level depended on an inflow rate of new orders and a reducing rate of shipments to customers. The form of the equation is similar to the previous one.

$$U_1 = U_0 + (\Delta t)(\text{Receipt of New Orders})_{01} - (\Delta t)(\text{Shipment Rate to Customers})_{01}$$

and

$$U_2 = U_1 + (\Delta t)(\text{Receipt of New Orders})_{12} - (\Delta t)(\text{Shipment Rate to Customers})_{12}$$

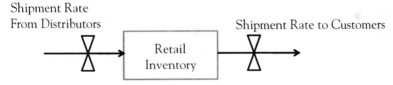

Shipment Rate
From Distributors   Shipment Rate to Customers

Figure 1.3. Illustration of rates and levels.

In the simulation, other equations are used to calculate the various rates. These rates typically depend on stocks or levels in the model. For example, in Forrester's model, the shipment rate to customers is dependent on the level of unfilled orders and the physical availability of inventory at the distributor, in this case expressed as the square root of the ratio of inventory to desired inventory. This is shown in Figure 1.4. *NOT CLEAR* In many cases, the desired inventory is a multiple of average demand, for example, 2 weeks of average sales or a month of sales. This averaging of sales is only one way in which time delays are included in the model. Other delays relate to purchasing processes, shipping times, and factory-production lead times.

System dynamics, by focusing on rates of change, feedback of information, and time delays, creates models that are difference equations for nonlinear differential equations. The stocks or levels are the state variables of the system. This approach enables the models to capture and replicate counterintuitive, and at times baffling, nonlinear behavior of systems, such as the bullwhip effect.

A simple model as shown in Figure 1.5 can also help illustrate model development and simulation. Whereas Forrester's model included three stages in a supply chain—factory, distributor, and retailer—this illustrative model includes only the retail sector. In the model, a retailer receives orders from customers. Shipments occur after a day or so of processing but only if inventory is available. In terms of assessing the inventory

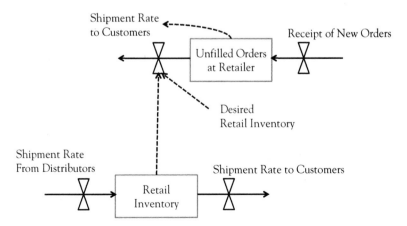

Figure 1.4. Determination of rates.

NOT A VERY CLEAR MODEL

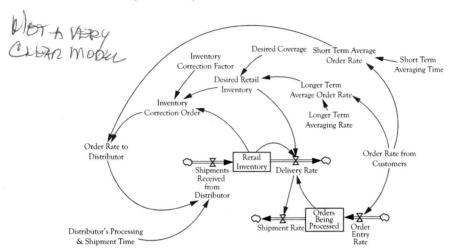

Figure 1.5. Simple feedback model.

position, the retailer compares the current inventory with a desired level of inventory. As inventory falls below the desired level, the retailer slows shipments to avoid running out of inventory. The retailer tries to maintain 2 weeks of average sales as the desired level of inventory, often termed a 2-week coverage. To be conservative in this determination, the retailer averages sales over a 4-week period, smoothing out any potentially misleading short-term fluctuations. The desired inventory is then twice this 4-week average. The retailer's order to the distributor is composed of the recent order rate plus a term that is proportional to the difference between the inventory and the desired inventory. This second component reflects a corrective feedback mechanism that drives inventory toward the desired level. This type of corrective action is a key feature of supply chain management and is widely reflected in the real world. The ability to capture this corrective feedback is a key aspect of system dynamics. It is assumed in this simple model that inventory is always available at the distributor so that after an average 4-week processing and shipment delay, the ordered shipments arrive at the retailer.

If the order rate from customers is constant at 10 per week, the model with the corrective feedback maintains a steady state, with desired inventory at 20, actual inventory also at 20, an order rate to the distributor of 10, and a delivery rate to the customers of 10. If, however, at the end of the fourth week, the customer weekly order rate is increased by 20% to 12 per week, it takes some time for the corrective actions to lead to a new balanced steady state. Figures 1.6 and 1.7 present the simulation results for this case.

Figure 1.6 presents the key rates in this simple model. As may be seen, the order rate from customers jumps from 10 to 12 at the end of week 4. The delivery rate to customers rises almost immediately to respond to the increased demand. The order rate to the distributor grows more slowly because of the delays in averaging the order rate but grows to 14 a week.

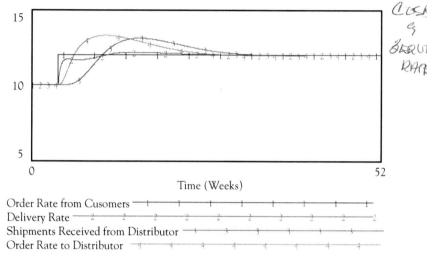

Order Rate from Cusomers
Delivery Rate
Shipments Received from Distributor
Order Rate to Distributor

Figure 1.6. Key rates.

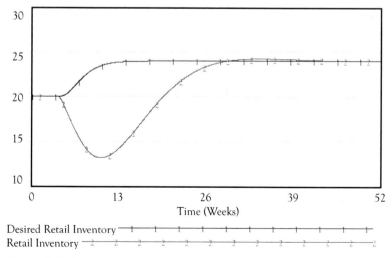

Desired Retail Inventory
Retail Inventory

Figure 1.7. Inventory.

This can be explained by reviewing Figure 1.7. As may be seen, retail inventory falls with the higher demand at the same time that the desired inventory is growing to reach twice the new level of average orders, again representing an inventory coverage of 2. The growing gap between retail inventory and desired retail inventory creates a larger and larger corrective order component. This is the reason for the high orders to the distributor. As may be seen in Figure 1.6, the shipments received from the distributor lag 4 weeks behind the orders to the distributor, but as the shipments arrive, retail inventory begins to recover and finally reaches the new desired level roughly half a year after the increase in orders.

Much of the dynamic behavior of this model depends on the strength of the feedback loop correcting the gap between actual and desired inventory. In the first simulation, it is assumed that the retailer is conservative in terms of the speed of closing the gap—specifically, that the gap would be closed over an 8-week period. The inventory correction factor is thus equal to one-eighth. This conservative closure rate would, of course, ease the flow of capital required to build inventory, but it also slows the response. In a second simulation, it is assumed that the retailer plans to close the gap in 4 weeks, so the inventory correction factor increases to one-fourth. The results of this more aggressive response are shown in Figures 1.8 and 1.9.

As may be seen in Figure 1.8, the increase in rates occurs faster and with greater strength. On the other hand, the rates overshoot the steady

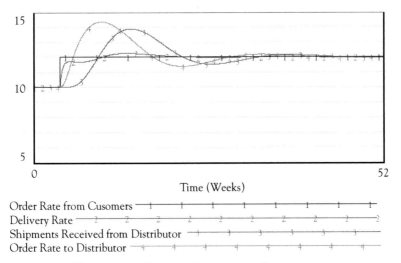

Figure 1.8. Key rates with 4-week inventory adjustment.

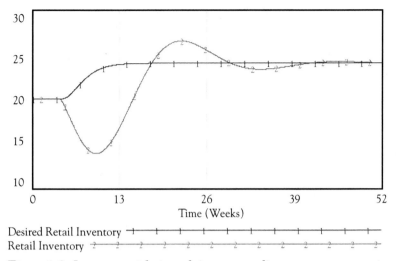

Desired Retail Inventory
Retail Inventory

Figure 1.9. Inventory with 4-week inventory adjustment.

state rates and then undershoot before stabilizing. The same may be seen for inventory in Figure 1.9, as the rates propel the actual inventory above and then below the desired level. This type of behavior is typical of systems with high *gain*—faster response but with a tendency to overshoot. Note that this complex behavior occurs with just a single sector represented in this model—retail. If distribution and production were added, the dynamics would be more actuated and exhibit a true bullwhip.

In managing complex systems, the speed and strength of corrective actions play a dominant role in system behavior over time. One might think that faster and stronger is always better, but often this approach produces results that are counterintuitive and unexpected. Figure 1.10 presents the order rate to the distributor for three cases of corrective response: an 8-week desired closure rate, the weakest and slowest response; a 4-week desired closure rate; and a 2-week desired closure rate, the fastest and strongest response.

As may be seen, the strongest response produces considerable overshoot and undershoot of the steady-state order rate. This fast response limits the decline in inventory, as seen in Figure 1.11, but again leads to overshoot of the inventory target.

The most favorable aspect of the strong and fast response is shown in Figure 1.12 in which customer orders being processed are kept at the

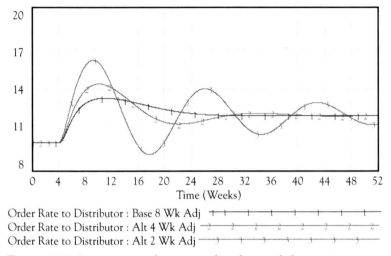

Order Rate to Distributor : Base 8 Wk Adj
Order Rate to Distributor : Alt 4 Wk Adj
Order Rate to Distributor : Alt 2 Wk Adj

Figure 1.10. Impacts on order rate to distributor of alternative inventory corrective actions.

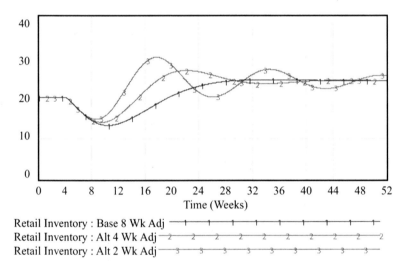

Retail Inventory : Base 8 Wk Adj
Retail Inventory : Alt 4 Wk Adj
Retail Inventory : Alt 2 Wk Adj

Figure 1.11. Impacts on retail inventory of alternative inventory corrective actions.

lowest level; in other words, customer orders are filled somewhat more promptly but at the cost of substantial variability introduced into the system. This type of self-imposed cycle of overstocking and understocking is not unusual in many supply chains.

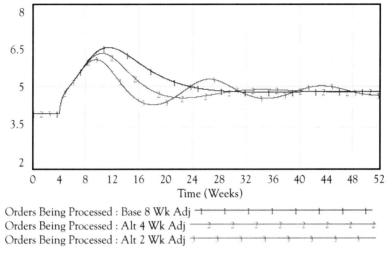

Orders Being Processed : Base 8 Wk Adj
Orders Being Processed : Alt 4 Wk Adj
Orders Being Processed : Alt 2 Wk Adj

Figure 1.12. Impacts on customer orders being processed of alternative inventory corrective actions.

This book explores the use of system dynamics models to better analyze and manage supply chains. In Chapter 2, a model is developed using a complex ordering mechanism that is of the type often embedded in enterprise-resource planning systems. One feature of the system examined is that, in addition to ordering new items, the system can order overhaul of used items to satisfy demand. In Chapter 3, a model is built involving a multitier and multichannel supply chain. In this model, eight components are produced in eight separate, three-tier supply chains before being assembled into the final product. In a system of this complexity, nonlinear behavior such as the bullwhip is readily observed. Chapter 4 demonstrates the evaluation of an optimal push-pull supply strategy using system dynamics. The performance of a static-based optimization solution is tested under dynamic conditions. In Chapter 5, a system dynamics supply chain model is used to determine life-cycle costs and, in particular, how improved reliability and reduced demand reduce life-cycle costs over an extended period. Investments in reliability are evaluated for return on investment and payback periods. Chapter 7 also explores the relationship between supply chains and life-cycle costs but focuses on the role of overhaul in reducing life-cycle costs. These models demonstrate the broad range of management activities that can be successfully investigated with system dynamics.

Although structural details of many models are presented in this book, the intent of the book is not to provide instruction on the building of system dynamics models or writing model equations. There are excellent books available for constructing system dynamics models, including *Industrial Dynamics* by Jay Forrester and *Business Dynamics* by John Sterman.[2] All the models presented in this book were developed using the simulation language Vensim by Ventana Systems. There is a useful modeling guide at their website, vensim.com. In addition, Craig W. Kirkwood at Arizona State University maintains a system dynamics resource page (http://www.public.asu.edu/~kirkwood/sysdyn/SDRes.htm) with a short tutorial for Vensim PLE (now updated to version 5). This book also does not attempt to serve as a textbook on supply chain management. An excellent resource for supply chain education is *Designing and Managing the Supply Chain: Concepts, Strategies and Case Studies* by my MIT colleagues David and Edith Simchi-Levi.

CHAPTER 2

The Dynamics of the Supply Process for High-Value Spare Parts

Introduction

Most modern supply chains function as a large-scale complex system with feedback controls at the nerve center. Data containing information on inventory levels, shipments due out, receipts due in, and so forth are "fed back" to the control center, and algorithms calculate and place orders that guide the system toward its desired or target state. This process is common in enterprise-resource planning (ERP) systems within large corporations. At the heart of many supply chains for high-value parts is a process known as the *requirements-determination system*, or the *supply-control study*.[1] This computer-based process is used to determine the number of recommended buys for new parts and the recommended number of parts to undergo repair and overhaul. The new purchases and the parts from overhaul constitute the sources for these parts and flow into inventory. The supply chain control system compares current levels of inventory, including due-ins and due-outs, with anticipated needs to calculate recommended buys and repairs. Since the procurement of new spares and the overhaul of damaged spares lead over time to changes in inventory, the system truly functions in a feedback-control fashion to manage the supply chain. Figure 2.1 presents an overview of this process.

In the computer-based process for determining recommended orders, many data elements are included in the calculations for recommended procurement buys and repair actions. Inputs to the requirements determination include average historical demand rates, production lead times

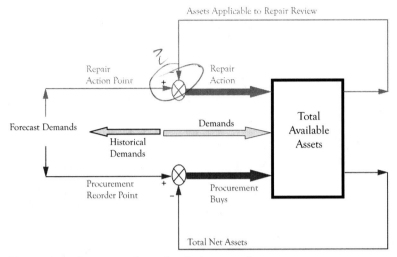

Figure 2.1. Overview of supply chain control process.

(PLTs) and repair lead times (RLTs), return and scrap rates of worn and damaged parts, inventory on hand, due-ins, due-outs, and desired safety levels. In the computerized requirements-determination process, the required data for a particular part such as a transmission or helicopter blade are extracted from product databases. Figure 2.2 presents the detailed supply chain and production data used to calculate the recommended procurement buys and repair actions for each high-value part.

The requirements-determination algorithms were embedded in a number of large government data systems such as the Commodity Command Standard System in the late 1960s and have been used continually since the early 1970s. As government agencies have moved to modern ERP systems such as SAP, these algorithms have migrated to these systems.

However, difficulties with the requirements-determination process and embedded algorithms and performance problems with the associated supply chains, have been reported on an ongoing basis for decades. Rosenman reported on the instabilities in the system and the frequently observed flip-flops in recommendations from one calculation to another.[2] Rosenman also noted an "uneasiness about how well this system might respond" to sudden changes in demand level.[3] The Government Accountability Office (GAO) has made frequent reports to Congress on the problems with the requirements-determination process and related

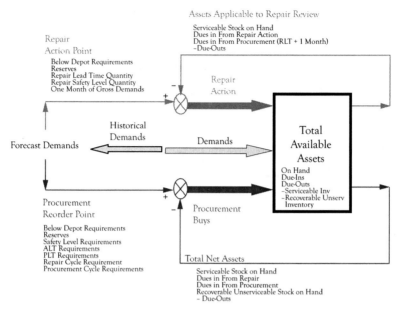

Figure 2.2. Data feeds used in supply chain management.

supply chain performance. These problems have been identified as arising from both the analytic process and its sensitivity to inaccurate data. In 1981, the GAO found substantial overstatement and understatement of requirements "because requirements computations were based on inaccurate delivery, administrative, and production lead-times."[4] In 1990, the GAO reported problems because item managers "accepted the inventory levels determined by a computer" and the "database that item managers relied upon to make retention decisions included inaccurate data and lacked some necessary data."[5] Moreover, the systems "were based on management processes, procedures, and concepts that have evolved over time but are largely outdated."[6] The GAO has identified management of inventory "as a high-risk area since 1990 due to ineffective and inefficient inventory systems and practices."[7] In addition, the GAO found that the government is experiencing difficulties estimating acquisition lead times to acquire spare parts, and this hinders "their ability to efficiently and effectively maintain spare parts inventories."[8] In short, the GAO has repeatedly stated that the government has "wasted billions of dollars on excess supplies, burdened itself with the need to maintain them, and failed to acquire the tools or expertise to manage them effectively."[9]

Because of the many problems in supply chain performance, especially the prevalence of shortages in high-value spare parts, it is important to (a) examine the impacts of the calculated recommendations of the supply-control study under a variety of time-varying demand conditions, (b) assess the impacts on supply chain performance of inaccurate data in the calculation of the recommended buys and overhaul, (c) determine any contribution of the process in the creation of a bullwhip effect, and (d) project supply chain performance in the face of real-world production-capacity constraints not included in the supply-control study.

Analytical Approach

Because of the feedback nature of the requirements-determination process, an appropriate technique for analyzing the impacts of the embedded control processes and investigating the resultant supply chain performance is a modeling and simulation approach developed at the MIT Sloan School of Management, termed *system dynamics*. System dynamics has been used to analyze supply chains from its very beginning as a modeling and simulation tool for policy analysis. Forrester's groundbreaking article in the *Harvard Business Review* demonstrated fundamental supply chain dynamic behavior, such as how small changes in retail sales and promotional activity can lead to large swings in factory production—the so-called bullwhip or Forrester effect.[10] Forrester also included a supply chain model and demonstrated various modes of behavior.[11] More recently, Sterman has addressed supply chains with several models and case studies.[12] Huang and Wang addressed the bullwhip effect in a closed-loop supply chain using a simple model based on Sterman's structure.[13] Schroeter and Spengler addressed the strategic management of spare parts in closed-loop supply chains.[14] Simchi-Levi, Kaminsky, and Simchi- Levi and Lee, Padmanabhan, and Whang analyzed the generation of bullwhip.[15] Finally, Angerhofer and Angelides presented a thorough discussion of system dynamics modeling in supply chain management.[16] The objective of the current research is to capture the actual algorithms of a government procurement process, embed this procurement or ordering process within a system dynamics supply chain model, and assess the impacts and performance of the process and supply chain.

Model Description

The model that has been developed is a detailed and dynamic version of the structure presented in the overview in Figure 2.1. The model is intended to simulate the behavior of the requirements-determination process and supply chain performance under a variety of demand and input assumptions. An overview of the major flows in the model is shown in Figure 2.3. Demand information flows to the control process to be used along with inventory data in the calculations that drive new production and overhaul actions. Parts that are removed are returned in a flow to the overhaul sites to be reworked. Orders for new parts flow to the commercial new production facility. If production capacity is available, then these orders enter production and, after a manufacturing or production lead time, flow into inventory. If production capacity is not available, then these orders enter a backlog and wait until capacity is available. Orders for overhaul are allocated between government depots and commercial overhaul facilities. If overhaul capacity is available and a returned part is also available, then overhaul is initiated. If capacity or a returned part is not available, then the order enters a backlog until there is both capacity and returned-part availability. Parts complete the overhaul process after an RLT and flow into the inventory system and then into use. The focus of the model is

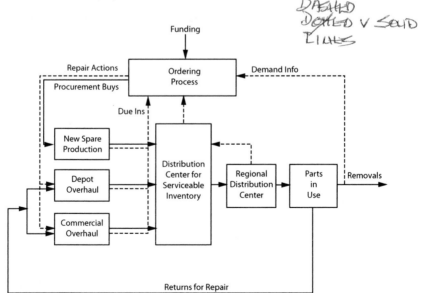

Figure 2.3. Overview of model flows.

to understand how the ordering process within the actual supply-control study affects the dynamics and performance of the real-world supply chain.

In the supply-control process, recommended orders for new parts are calculated as the difference between the procurement reorder point (i.e., the minimum amount of stock that should be available to meet demands until the next scheduled order) and the total net assets. The recommended order is the difference between these values plus the procurement cycle requirement—the amount of inventory necessary to meet demands until the next scheduled order (see Figure 2.4).

In this process, the total net assets are calculated by summing the available inventories and the items due in from the procurement and repair processes and subtracting the number of items due out. This is shown in Figure 2.4. The procurement reorder point is determined by the necessary safety levels and inventory requirements to sustain inventory levels through the next scheduled purchase. This second level of data input to the controller is shown in Figure 2.5, where the new spares completion rate flows into the serviceable inventory and new spares work in progress (WIP) and orders awaiting production start are components in the calculation of due-ins from procurement.

Figure 2.6 presents the third level of variables used in the calculation of recommended procurement action. Note in Figure 2.6 that the procurement reorder point is strongly determined by average historical demands. In the actual process, this averaging is typically for 24 months.

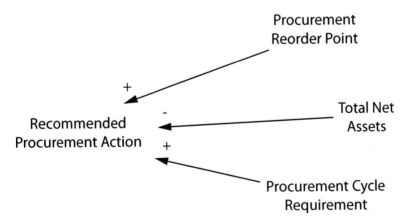

Figure 2.4. Recommended procurement action.

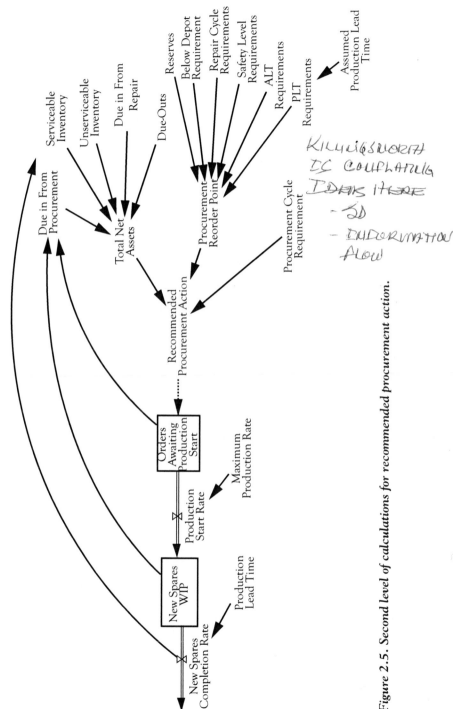

Figure 2.5. Second level of calculations for recommended procurement action.

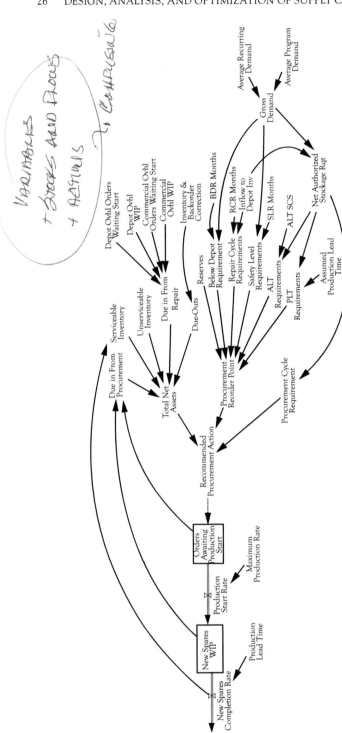

Figure 2.6. Echelons of variables in the procurement ordering system.

The calculation of the recommended repair action is somewhat different from the calculation for recommended purchase of new spares. The key difference is that repair and overhaul can proceed only if there is a worn or damaged part available on which to work. This availability is determined by the effectiveness of the reverse logistics flow (there is an assumed loss rate) and the percentage that must be scrapped due to excessive wear or damage. The supply-control process calculates a maximum recommended repair action by taking the difference between the repair action point and the assets applicable to repair review. This maximum recommended repair is then compared to the on-hand inventory of unserviceable inventory, and the minimum of these two variables is then the recommended repair action (see Figure 2.7 and the glossary at the end of this chapter).

Once a repair is recommended, the cost of the repair is calculated to determine if sufficient funding is available. With available funding, the repair quantity then may be allocated for depot overhaul, commercial overhaul sites, or both. After an item has been repaired, it is added to the serviceable inventory and the calculation of assets applicable to repair review. The second tier of variables used in the calculation of the maximum recommended repair action is shown in Figure 2.8. Feedbacks from the repair actions to inventory and due-ins are illustrated as dashed lines in Figure 2.8.

As shown in Figure 2.3, the model includes a central inventory distribution center as well as a regional distribution center. The

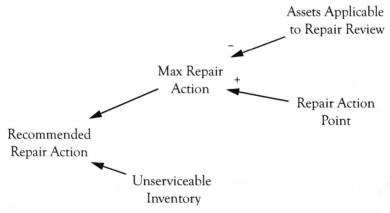

Figure 2.7. Recommended repair action.

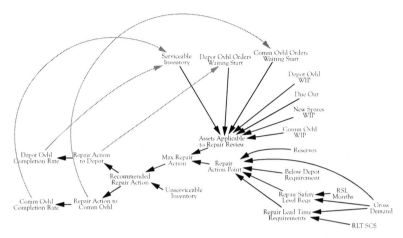

Figure 2.8. Echelons of variables in the current repair ordering system.

requirements-determination process described previously replenishes the central inventory of serviceable parts. This central inventory then replenishes the regional inventory. The regional center places orders to the central distribution center as shown in Figure 2.9. This section of the model is similar to the structure incorporated in other system dynamics, supply chain–related models in which desired inventory coverage is based on historical demand.[17]

Finally, Figure 2.10 presents an overview of the closed-loop, reverse-logistics process in the model. Part removals (i.e., demands) are generated based on the number of parts in use, the monthly hours of operation, and a failure rate per part per hour of monthly use. Some of these removed parts are lost or are too damaged to be repaired. The remainder is returned for close inspection and evaluation. Some of these parts are scrapped. The remainder is then divided between commercial and government depot overhaul facilities. These are then matched with a repair order and on completion of the repair are ready for reissue.

Analysis and Simulation Results

Key objectives of the analysis were to (a) ascertain the robustness of the requirements-determination and supply-control processes in facing

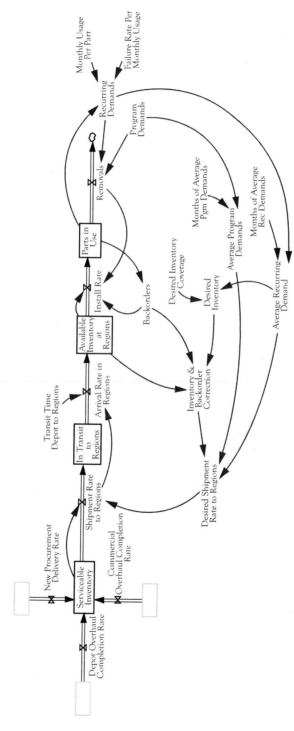

Figure 2.9. Ordering process from regions to central inventory.

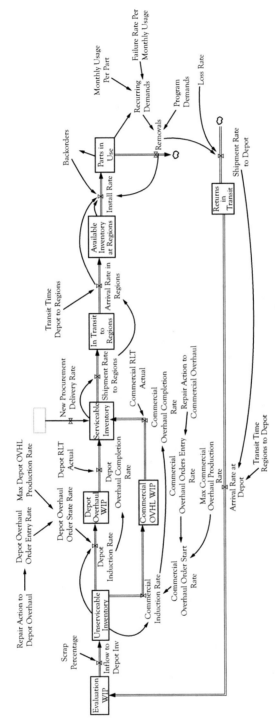

Figure 2.10. Demand and return process.

alternative demand profiles, (b) assess the potential of the requirements-determination process for creating bullwhip in the supply chain, (c) determine the sensitivity of the supply control to inaccurate data, and (d) evaluate the impacts of real-world production and overhaul capacity constraints. The model described has been parameterized for a number of specific high-value parts and has been used to simulate the behavior and performance of the supply-control process and the supply chain for these particular parts. The following cases are presented with a simulation time covering 2001–2012:   *CALIBRATION*
OF MODEL

Case 1. Constant demand

Case 2. Ramp-up in demand beginning in 2003

Case 3. Oscillation in demand

Case 4. Error in assumed and actual PLT in 2004

Case 5. Ramp-up in demand in 2003 with production constraints

Case 6. Ramp-up (2003) and ramp-down (2009) in demand with production constraints

Case 7. Ramp-up (2003) and ramp-down (2009) in demand with production constraints and error in assumed and actual PLT

Cases 1 and 2 were used to both validate the model and verify that the requirements-determination process generated appropriate orders in response to constant demand and a near step ramp-up in demand for a higher constant level. Case 3 was conducted to determine if the governmental computerized-ordering process and the related supply chain exhibited the bullwhip effect. Because numerous reports[18] have indicated that certain data, such as production lead time, used in the ordering process are often incorrect, case 4 investigates the impact of incorrect production lead time on the ordering process and supply chain performance. Moreover, because the governmental ordering process does not include the potential for production-capacity constraints, case 5 examines the behavior of the supply-control process and the ability of the system to meet rising demand in the presence of capacity constraints. Finally, cases 6 and 7 examine "real-world" scenarios involving shifting demand, production constraints, and data errors.

Case 1 assumes a constant demand of 14 parts per month. For certain high-value parts, this is a realistic monthly demand. These are not high-volume, consumer-product supply chains. Constant demand provides one test of validation and offers a suitable base case for comparison to subsequent cases. It is assumed in case 1 that there are no production-capacity constraints. Production lead time is assumed to be 22 months and RLT is assumed to be 11 months—typical values for this type of part within the government supply chain. It is important to note that the PLT and RLT assumed for the requirements determination are equal to the actual values. No errors are assumed in input assumptions. Simulation output for case 1 is presented in Figures 2.11 to 2.14. Inventories remain at a constant level throughout the simulation time period; as items are removed and demands are generated, orders are created and items are

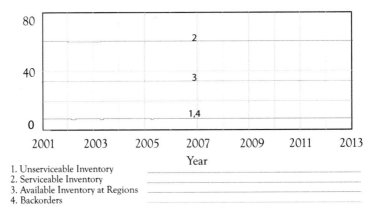

Figure 2.11. Case 1: Inventories with constant demand.

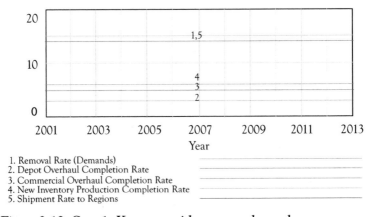

Figure 2.12. Case 1: Key rates with constant demand.

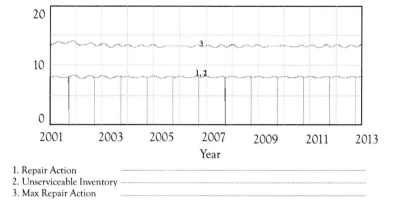

1. Repair Action
2. Unserviceable Inventory
3. Max Repair Action

Figure 2.13. Case 1: Repair action with constant demand.

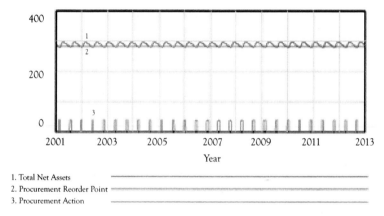

1. Total Net Assets
2. Procurement Reorder Point
3. Procurement Action

Figure 2.14. Case 1: Procurement action with constant demand.

replaced regularly, establishing equilibrium within the system (see Figure 2.11). In a similar manner, the key rates within the model remain constant (see Figure 2.12). The completion rates of the two overhaul sectors combined with the new production completion rate are equivalent to the removals; hence, demands are met as necessary. Note also that the shipment rate to regions overlaps with the removal rate in Figure 2.12, showing that demands are being met as needed. The recommended repair quantity is limited by the amount of unserviceable inventory on hand, as shown in Figure 2.13. Of the 14 parts removed monthly, it is assumed that 85% are returned for repair, and of those, 35% are scrapped as irreparable. This constrains the repair action to roughly eight per month.

Unserviceable inventory coincides with the repair action in this graph, while the max repair action value is much higher (see the glossary at the end of the chapter for definitions). Meanwhile, the recommended procurement action does not have such a limitation, and procurement orders are placed regularly according to the procurement cycle requirement (see Figure 2.14). As parts are removed from serviceable inventory, total net assets decline, and eventually the value dips below the procurement reorder point. A buy is generated at this point, and the increase in the due-ins from procurement increases the total net assets above the reorder point, and the buy process is halted. Even in the face of constant demand, the process creates a periodic buy action. This is shown in Figure 2.14.

It is important to note at this point that both the recommended procurement action and the max repair action are determined as the difference of two large numbers. This makes the result very sensitive to noisy data. (It is well known that the distribution of a difference of two normally distributed variants X and Y with means and variances $[\mu_x, \sigma_x^2]$ and $[\mu_y, \sigma_y^2]$, respectively, is given by another normal distribution having mean $\mu_{x-y} = \mu_x - \mu_y$ and variance $[\sigma_{x-y}^2 = \sigma_x^2 + \sigma_y^2]$ (http://mathworld.wolfram .com).)[19] For example, in Figure 2.13, the procurement reorder point (being demand driven) is constant at 280. The total net assets figure varies between 278 and 295 with an average value of roughly 286. Thus the mean of the difference is about 6. If the two large numbers were each to have a standard deviation of 30 (i.e., roughly 10% of their means), then the difference—the recommended procurement action—would have a mean of 6 with a standard deviation of roughly 42. It is no wonder that Rosenman noted instabilities in the requirements-determination process very early in its usage.[20] This is an important finding within the modeling process.

Case 2 examines a ramping-up of demand over a 12-month period from 14 parts per month to 18 per month. All other assumptions are identical to case 1. In this example, the increase in demand by four units per month over the course of the year 2003 results in the depletion of serviceable inventory (see Figure 2.15). During this time, when serviceable inventories are depleted, back orders build. The requirements-determination process and supply-control system do lead to inventory recovery, but it takes approximately 2 years to work off all the back orders and to begin to build reserve-inventory levels once

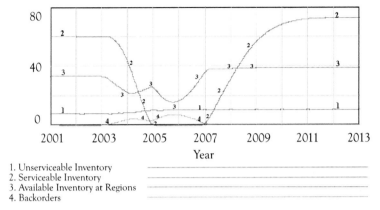

1. Unserviceable Inventory
2. Serviceable Inventory
3. Available Inventory at Regions
4. Backorders

Figure 2.15. Case 2: Inventories with ramp-up in demand in 2003.

again. The delays in the system are apparent in the key rates graph in
Figure 2.16. Demand begins to increase at the beginning of 2003, but
the production-completion rates do not begin to rise until 2004. This
is due to the acquisition lead time, the production lead time, and the
RLT. The supply-control process uses new procurement as a primary
method of meeting increased demands due to the limited availability of unserviceable items on hand for overhaul. The unserviceable
inventory coincides with the repair action again in the graph in Figure 2.17. Although the recommended repair (i.e., max repair action)
is much higher, there is not enough repairable stock on hand to meet
this recommendation. The procurement action, on the other hand,
continues to ensure the total net assets on hand do not dip far below

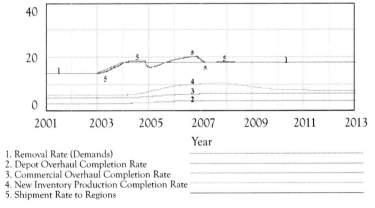

1. Removal Rate (Demands)
2. Depot Overhaul Completion Rate
3. Commercial Overhaul Completion Rate
4. New Inventory Production Completion Rate
5. Shipment Rate to Regions

Figure 2.16. Case 2: Key rates with ramp-up in demand in 2003.

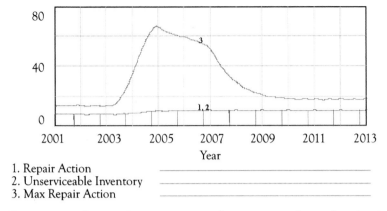

1. Repair Action
2. Unserviceable Inventory
3. Max Repair Action

Figure 2.17. Case 2: Repair action with ramp-up in demand in 2003.

the procurement reorder point, which increases as demand rises in 2003 (see Figure 2.18). Accordingly, the periodic behavior is seen again in this case. It is important to note that cases 1 and 2 verify that the recommended procurement and repair actions of the requirements-determination process are appropriate and do lead to the necessary orders in the case of constant demand and a step-up in demand.

Case 3 is designed to examine whether the requirements-determination process leads to bullwhip behavior in the supply chain. The input assumptions creating demand for parts removal are assumed to be sinusoidal with periods of 2, 4, and 8 years. The average demand is the same as case 1 at 14 units per month. The sine waves oscillate

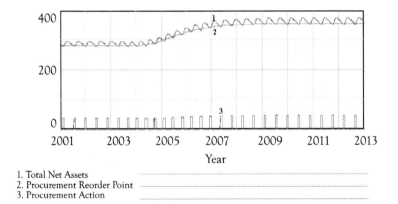

1. Total Net Assets
2. Procurement Reorder Point
3. Procurement Action

Figure 2.18. Case 2: Procurement with ramp-up in demand in 2003.

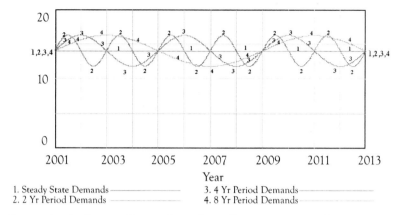

Figure 2.19. Case 3: Demands with oscillation variance of 20% in varying time periods.

±20% around 14 units per month (see Figure 2.19). As in the prior two cases, this case assumes no production-capacity constraints (as always, repair is constrained by availability of unserviceable parts), and input assumptions for PLT and RLT are equal to actual lead times. With these assumptions, the new spare production rate becomes extremely volatile for the longer fluctuation periods, varying as much as 40% in the 8-year oscillation period (see Figure 2.20). As a result, the amount of unserviceable inventory returning to be refurbished also becomes

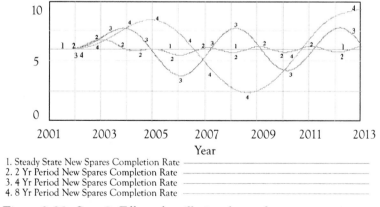

Figure 2.20. Case 3: Effect of oscillating demands on new spares completion rate.

variable, with drastic spikes occurring primarily in the 4- and 8-year cycles (see Figure 2.21). Due to this volatility within the levels of unserviceable inventory, depot and commercial overhaul rates also fluctuate accordingly (see Figures 2.22 and 2.23). In the 4- and 8-year oscillation period cases, these overhaul completion rates vary by as much as 30%. The highly varying production and overhaul rates cause significant changes in the serviceable inventory available for issue (see Figure 2.24). At times, as a result of this bullwhip effect, there is no serviceable

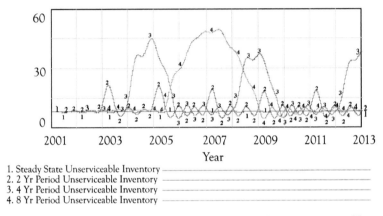

1. Steady State Unserviceable Inventory
2. 2 Yr Period Unserviceable Inventory
3. 4 Yr Period Unserviceable Inventory
4. 8 Yr Period Unserviceable Inventory

Figure 2.21. Case 3: Effect of oscillating demands on unserviceable inventory.

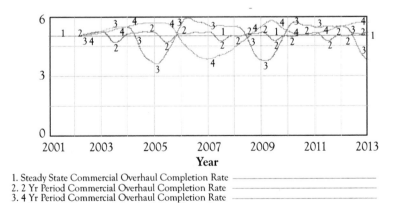

1. Steady State Commercial Overhaul Completion Rate
2. 2 Yr Period Commercial Overhaul Completion Rate
3. 4 Yr Period Commercial Overhaul Completion Rate
4. 8 Yr Period Commercial Overhaul Completion Rate

Figure 2.22. Case 3: Effect of oscillating demands on commercial overhaul completion rate.

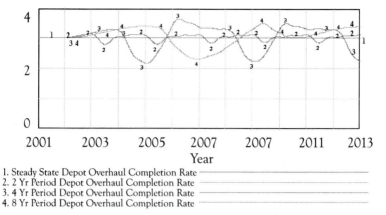

1. Steady State Depot Overhaul Completion Rate
2. 2 Yr Period Depot Overhaul Completion Rate
3. 4 Yr Period Depot Overhaul Completion Rate
4. 8 Yr Period Depot Overhaul Completion Rate

Figure 2.23. Case 3: Effect of oscillating demands on depot overhaul completion rate.

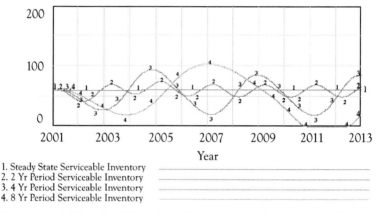

1. Steady State Serviceable Inventory
2. 2 Yr Period Serviceable Inventory
3. 4 Yr Period Serviceable Inventory
4. 8 Yr Period Serviceable Inventory

Figure 2.24. Case 3: Effect of oscillating demands on serviceable inventory.

inventory available in the 8-year oscillation cycle. Hence the available inventory varies by as much as 100%. This case with no production constraints clearly demonstrates that the algorithms of the supply-control process lead to bullwhip effects within the government supply chain. In the event that production constraints are considered, this behavior is still readily apparent. Although constraints are present in the real system, the current government ordering process does not take these constraints into consideration when recommending a purchase or an overhaul. The impacts of this are investigated in case 5.

Another situation that causes potential for significant problems within the government ordering system is data inaccuracies. This is especially true for production lead times. Case 4 examines this issue using two examples in which the actual production lead time increases from 22 months to 32 months in 2004. This situation developed for many high-value spare parts due to rapidly rising lead times for certain raw materials such as aerospace steels and titanium. In the first example, the assumed PLT in the requirements-determination calculation remains at 22 months for the entire period even though the actual PLT jumps to 32 months during 2004. In the second example, the assumption in the government ordering system is corrected a year later and increases to 32 months in 2005. (This so-called learning case would almost certainly be the result of human intervention in the process because the data process itself would take much longer to identify the increase.)

When the production lead time increases, the new production completion rate immediately declines (see Figure 2.25). If the government ordering system does not adjust the error in assumed PLT, the system continues to place orders with the assumption that the new spares will be delivered much sooner than will actually occur. As a result, the new spare production completion remains depressed. If the government ordering system adjusts its expected lead time accordingly, then the system compensates by ordering additional new parts, creating an increase in the new

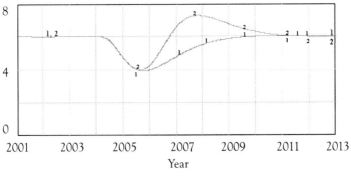

1. Non-Learning New Spares Completion Rate
2. Learning New Spares Completion Rate

Figure 2.25. Case 4: Effect of increase in PLT on new production completion rate.

spare completion rate (see Figure 2.26). Over time, this increase in orders and new spare production enables a recovery of inventory to begin (see Figure 2.27).

Another problem that arose in supply chains for high-value spare parts during 2005 and 2006 was a rapid rise in back orders arising from capacity constraints in the production of new parts and in overhaul. The requirements-determination process was generating orders, but manufacturing could not keep pace. Case 5 examines supply chain performance under such production constraints. Case 5 assumes the same

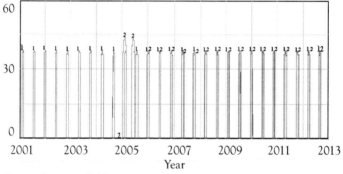

1. Non-Learning Recommended Procurement Action
2. Learning Recommended Procurement Action

Figure 2.26. Case 4: Effect of increase in PLT on recommended procurement.

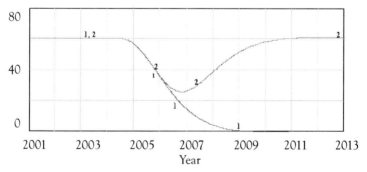

1. Non-Learning Serviceable Inventory

2. Learning Serviceable Inventory

Figure 2.27. Case 4. Effect of increase in PLT on serviceable inventory.

increased demand assumptions as Case 2 but also assumes a maximum depot overhaul capacity of 6 parts per month, a maximum commercial overhaul capacity of 10 parts per month, and a maximum new production capacity of 8 parts per month. (These constraints in practice were typically created by lack of tooling and labor.) Under these assumptions, back orders increase, and inventories are depleted and only recover after 2 to 3 years as may be seen in Figure 2.28. Both new spare production rate and overhaul rate increase to their maximums and remain at those levels for the simulation period (see Figure 2.29). The recommended repair action substantially exceeds both the maximum overhaul capacity and the availability of unserviceable parts to undergo overhaul. Repair action is still limited by the unserviceable inventory on hand, which coincides with the repair action on the graph (see Figure 2.30). In Figure 2.31, the procurement reorder point increases in response to the increased demand, and orders for new spares also increase. Delivery, however, is constrained by the production limits, and supply chain performance suffers.

The model is now being used to examine and develop supply chain strategies under alternative assumptions for future demand rates as well as changes in other conditions such as production lead times. Case 6 maintains the same assumptions as the previous case, but in addition to ramping up the demand

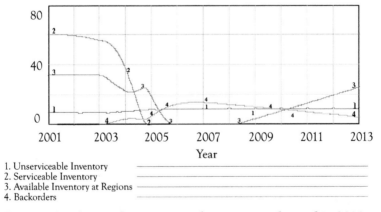

1. Unserviceable Inventory
2. Serviceable Inventory
3. Available Inventory at Regions
4. Backorders

Figure 2.28. Case 5: Inventories with ramp-up in demand in 2003 with overhaul and production constraints.

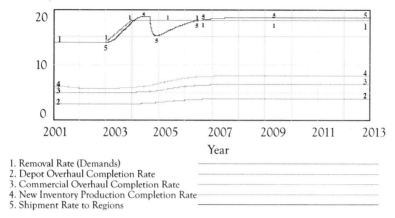

1. Removal Rate (Demands)
2. Depot Overhaul Completion Rate
3. Commercial Overhaul Completion Rate
4. New Inventory Production Completion Rate
5. Shipment Rate to Regions

Figure 2.29. Case 5: Key rates with ramp-up in demand in 2003 with overhaul and production constraints.

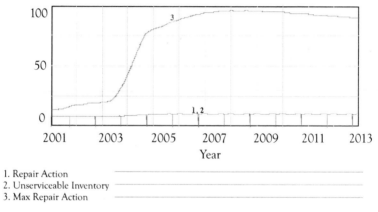

1. Repair Action
2. Unserviceable Inventory
3. Max Repair Action

Figure 2.30. Case 5: Repair action with ramp-up in demand in 2003 with overhaul and production constraints.

in 2003, demand is reduced to the 2003 levels over a 2-year period beginning in mid-2009. As demand ramps down in 2010, the system overshoots. Back orders are rapidly worked off, inventory grows rapidly, and an excess of stock is created (see Figure 2.32). This is due to both the long production lead times and the averaging of demand in calculating the requirements and recommended orders. As may be seen in Figure 2.33, production and overhaul completion rates only begin to decline some time after demand has dropped.

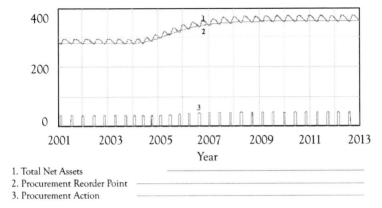

1. Total Net Assets
2. Procurement Reorder Point
3. Procurement Action

Figure 2.31. Case 5: Procurement with ramp-up in demand in 2003 with overhaul and production constraints.

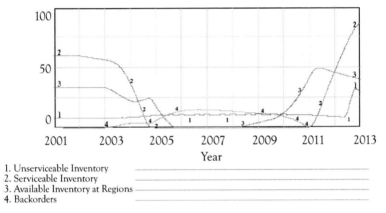

1. Unserviceable Inventory
2. Serviceable Inventory
3. Available Inventory at Regions
4. Backorders

Figure 2.32. Case 6: Inventories with ramp-up (2003) and ramp-down (2009) in demand with overhaul and production constraints.

When the demand decreases and inventory builds, new procurement orders take place less frequently (see Figure 2.35).

Another "real-world" case with interesting implications combines several of the previous assumptions. In case 7, demand levels begin at 14 per month, ramp up to 18 per month in 2003, and decline to the original levels starting in mid-2009. Production lead time begins at 22 months and ramps up to 32 months in 2004. The system continues to assume a PLT of 22 months until 2005, when it "learns" of the increase and ramps up to the equivalent of the actual value, 32 months. Case 7 also includes

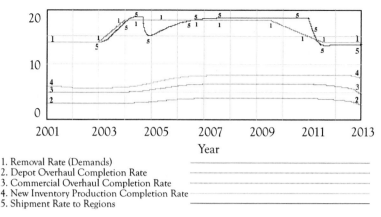

1. Removal Rate (Demands)
2. Depot Overhaul Completion Rate
3. Commercial Overhaul Completion Rate
4. New Inventory Production Completion Rate
5. Shipment Rate to Regions

Figure 2.33. Case 6: Key rates with ramp-up (2003) and ramp-down (2009) in demand with overhaul and production constraints.

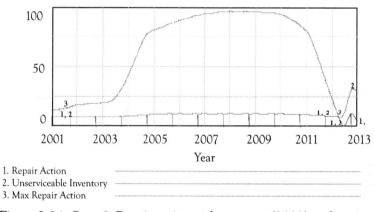

1. Repair Action
2. Unserviceable Inventory
3. Max Repair Action

Figure 2.34. Case 6: Repair action with ramp-up (2003) and ramp-down (2009) in demand with overhaul and production constraints.

production and overhaul constraints, limiting depot overhaul to 6 items a month, commercial overhaul to 10 items a month, and new procurement to 8 items a month. The totality of these assumptions very closely matches the actual situation in 2003 and 2004. Due to all the limitations on the ordering process, inventories immediately drop in 2003 and back orders ensue, picking up significant growth in 2004, upon the onset of the error in PLT (see Figure 2.36). The increase in PLT primarily affects the production completion rate and, coupled with the capacity constraints,

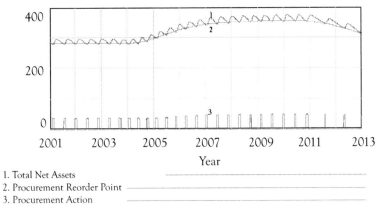

1. Total Net Assets
2. Procurement Reorder Point
3. Procurement Action

Figure 2.35. Case 6: Procurement with ramp-up (2003) and ramp-down (2009) in demand with overhaul and production constraints.

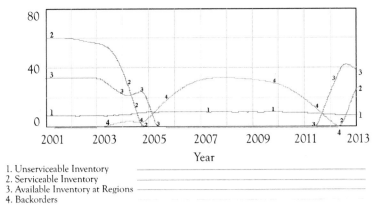

1. Unserviceable Inventory
2. Serviceable Inventory
3. Available Inventory at Regions
4. Backorders

Figure 2.36. Case 7: Inventories with ramp-up (2003) and ramp-down (2009) in demand with overhaul and production constraints and an error in estimated production lead time with learning.

limits production and, ultimately, shipment rates to the regions (see Figure 2.37). Similary, the constraints on overhaul production limits that source of output (see Figure 2.38). Procurement action is also impacted (see Figure 2.39) and the recovery of the inventory levels until 2011.

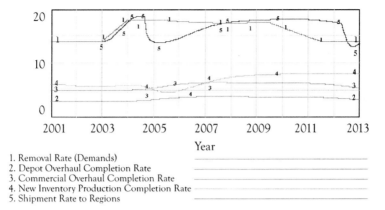

1. Removal Rate (Demands)
2. Depot Overhaul Completion Rate
3. Commercial Overhaul Completion Rate
4. New Inventory Production Completion Rate
5. Shipment Rate to Regions

Figure 2.37. Case 7: Key rates with ramp-up (2003) and ramp-down (2009) in demand with overhaul and production constraints and an error in estimated production lead time with learning.

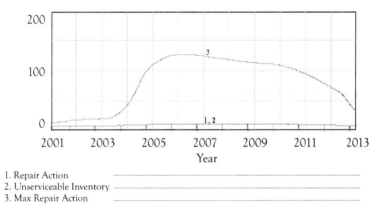

1. Repair Action
2. Unserviceable Inventory
3. Max Repair Action

Figure 2.38. Case 7: Repair action with ramp-up (2003) and ramp-down (2009) in demand with overhaul and production constraints and an error in estimated production lead time with learning.

Conclusions

Procurement systems for high-value spare parts have a long history of problems, often being plagued by both excess inventory and shortages. A process used in the calculation for recommended purchases of new spares and for overhauled parts is at the heart of many of these computerized processes. These algorithms have been embedded in a system dynamics model of the supply chain. This modeling effort has revealed that the

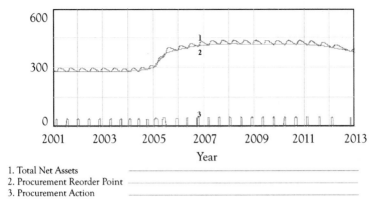

Figure 2.39. Case 7: Procurement with ramp-up (2003) and ramp-down (2009) in demand with overhaul and production constraints and an error in estimated production lead time with learning.

requirements-determination process or supply-control study has several very troubling characteristics. First, recommended orders are calculated as the difference of two large numbers. This formulation requires extreme accuracy of data for the process to be stable and to function appropriately. Second, data accuracy continues to plague these systems, and the system is shown to be highly sensitive to inaccurate data such as the production lead time and the RLT. Third, the process and the related supply chain are shown to exhibit substantial bullwhip effect in the face of varying demands. The tendency to bullwhip, coupled with data inaccuracies, can create, and has created in the past, considerable problems in inventory management with substantial swings in available inventory.

Glossary

Definitions

ALT requirements: Amount of stock necessary to meet expected demands during the administrative lead time (i.e., the time from initiation of the contract until it is awarded).

assets applicable to repair review: The amount of inventory that is in a condition suitable for issuance through the time it takes to repair unserviceable inventory.

below depot requirements: Quantity of inventory stored at selected forward sites.

due in from procurement: The amount of inventory purchased on contract but not yet received in the inventory.

due in from repair: The amount of inventory inducted into repair programs but not yet received in the inventory.

due out: Back orders.

max repair action: The maximum quantity of an item that may need to be repaired per month.

PLT requirements: Amount of stock necessary to meet expected demands during the production lead time (i.e., the time beginning at the awarding of a contract until a product is delivered).

procurement cycle requirement: The approximate time between scheduled purchases.

procurement reorder point: The minimum stock needed to meet demands until the next scheduled purchase.

repair action point: The total number of assets required for issue during the repair lead time.

repair cycle requirements: Quantity of inventory held to fill orders while other assets are being repaired.

repair lead time requirements: Amount of stock necessary to meet expected demands during the repair lead time (i.e., the time required to repair unserviceable inventory).

serviceable inventory: Inventory that is in condition to be issued for use.

total net assets: The total amount of stock on hand and due in.

unserviceable inventory: Inventory that is not in suitable condition to be issued for use but is in repairable condition.

CHAPTER 3

The Dynamics of Multitier, Multichannel Supply Chains

Introduction

Manufacturing has changed. Companies that were once known as automakers or aircraft manufacturers are now more properly viewed as integrators or assemblers. Parts and major subassemblies are now outsourced and are planned to arrive at the assembly plant just in time for integration into cars, airplanes, and other major products. Consider, for example, the Boeing 787 Dreamliner. The wing comes from Japan; the movable trailing edge of the wing is produced in Australia; the fixed and movable leading edge of the wing is produced in Oklahoma; the wing tips are produced in Korea; the center fuselage is made in Italy; the landing gear is made in the UK; and the landing gear doors are made in Canada.[1] Automakers and electronic-equipment manufacturers have similar extended supply chains. Subassemblies and major components come from a vast geographic network that is both broad and deep.

In these supply chains, major subassemblies are shipped to the Original Equipment Manufacturers (OEM) by hundreds of first-tier suppliers, but these first-tier companies are just the tip of the supply chain iceberg. For each major component or subassembly, there is a multitier supply chain that may extend back, for example, from a first-tier precision machining company, to a second-tier casting company, to a third-tier raw-material provider. Moreover, each major subassembly, such as a transmission or landing gear, is made from multiple parts, each provided by a separate channel through a multitier supply chain. Thus most, if not all, major subassemblies are the product of a multitier, multichannel supply chain. It is important to note that in the supply chains for government aviation parts, overhaul is a major source of supply. When damaged parts are returned for overhaul, they require some of the components from the multichannel, multitier supply chains. Overhaul thus creates demands in addition to those of the new production process. Shortages of components thus affect both new production and overhaul of high-value aviation parts.

Performance problems often arise in the lower tiers of these supply chains. For example, in 2004, the lead time for both aerospace steels and titanium grew from roughly 3 months to more than a year. Lead time for titanium continued to grow and reached roughly 70 weeks in 2005 and 2006. These developments threw the supply chains for aviation assemblies such as transmissions and landing gears into disarray. In a somewhat similar manner, the resurgence of the aviation industry has led to growth in orders that exceeded the production capacity of many lower-tier suppliers, and back orders are often common. For example, demands for aerospace fasteners recently exceeded production capacities. As a result of delays in receiving raw material and capacity constraints, inventories of many high-value spare parts for government aviation have declined to very low levels and have had difficulty recovering. Supply chain issues of one type or another have delayed both the Airbus 380 and the Boeing 787. While numerous studies have suggested a reformation of the government supply process that was implemented decades ago,[2] the same underlying process and associated problems tend to plague the system in place today.

A system dynamics model was developed to investigate the dynamics of multitier, multichannel supply chains providing high-value aviation parts. The objectives were to examine the impacts of the ordering process under a variety of time-varying demand conditions; assess the impacts on supply chain performance of inaccurate data in the calculation of the recommended buys and overhaul; examine the bullwhip effect in the multitier, multichannel supply chain; assess the potential for cross-coupling of problems among the multiple channels; and examine supply chain performance in the face of production capacity constraints not included in the supply requirements-determination process of the government.

Model Description

The overall supply chain system providing high-value aviation spare parts is shown in overview in Figure 3.1. This supply chain extends from raw material to final customer. Demand arises from aircraft located in four regions of the world. Demand in each region is driven by the number of aircraft in the region, monthly flight hours, and failure rate per part per flight hour. Each region has an inventory of key spare parts, and these inventories are replenished from a central-distribution inventory. Supply of parts comes from three sources: production of new items, commercial overhaul of damaged parts, and government depot overhaul of damaged parts. Each type of production requires that a number of parts be integrated into the major subassembly. In general, the overhaul process requires fewer component parts than new part production.

Each component part is produced through a three-tier supply chain. Each of these chains typically has a different manufacturing time at each tier, and each channel has a different total production time. The overall supply process is managed in a feedback fashion by the government's ordering or requirements-determination process. This process is at the heart of many government and defense supply chains for high-value parts.[3] This computerized process is used to determine the recommended buys for new parts and the recommended number of parts to undergo repair and overhaul. The supply chain control system compares current

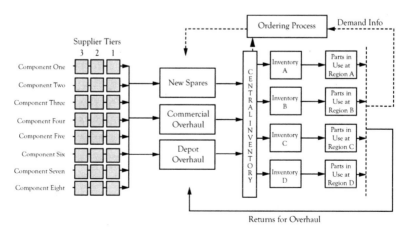

Figure 3.1. Overview of the multitier, multichannel supply chain model.

levels of inventory, including due-ins and due-outs, with anticipated needs to calculate recommended buys and repairs. Since the procurement of new spares and the overhaul of damaged spares leads over time to changes in inventory, the system truly functions in a feedback-control fashion to manage the supply chain.[4]

Figure 3.2 provides a more detailed view of the flows present in the model. It is important to note that many, if not the majority, of these aviation supply chains for high-value government spare parts operate in a sequential fashion, with little information sharing and little risk taking within the supply chains. For example, the government will request a proposal from the OEM to provide a certain number of the major assemblies. The OEM will respond with a proposal and, after negotiation, will be awarded a contract. The OEM will then request a proposal from the first-tier suppliers to provide their components. A proposal will be submitted and negotiated, and the OEM will award a contract to the first-tier suppliers. These first-tier suppliers will then turn to the second tiers and repeat the process. The second tiers will only then place an order with the third tiers for, in many cases, the necessary raw material. Hence many months can pass before the order for raw materials is placed, and recently, many months then pass before the raw material is received. This sequential structure is built within the model. Moreover, the first-tier, second-tier, and third-tier suppliers are very risk averse and maintain essentially zero inventory of both their inputs and their outputs. Purchasing of inputs and production of outputs only occur in the presence of a contract or purchase order.

Several levels of calculation are incorporated into the supply chain control center to determine recommended buys and repairs.[5] This computerized requirements-determination process is embedded in many government supply databases. Within the determination process, the recommended procurement action for new spare parts is calculated by taking the difference between the procurement reorder point and the total available net assets, and then adding the procurement cycle requirement, the inventory necessary to meet demands until the next scheduled order (see Figure 3.3). Total net assets are calculated from due-ins from procurement and repair plus inventories, less due-outs. The procurement reorder point is based on reserves and safety levels. Orders that are placed with the OEM enter production subject to a maximum production rate

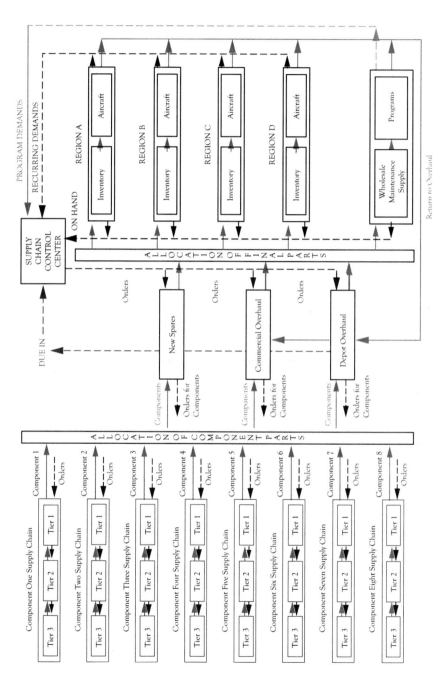

Figure 3.2. Detailed overview of model flows.

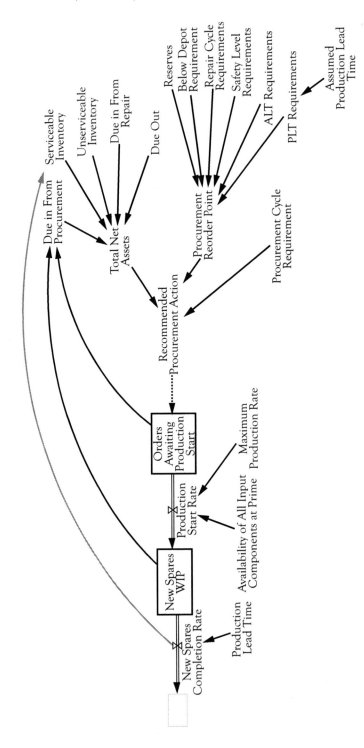

Figure 3.3. Recommended new spares procurement action.

and availability of all required components. Production is completed after a manufacturing lead time. These parts then flow into serviceable inventory.

In a separate calculation, the recommended repair action is determined. It must be noted that repair and overhaul can be conducted only if there is a damaged part available to be overhauled. The maximum recommended repair action is calculated by subtracting the assets available for repair, including overhaul and procurement work in progress less due-outs, from the repair action point, calculated with reserve levels and safety requirements. This repair action point is largely driven by historical demands. The maximum recommended repair action, however, is then limited by the unserviceable inventory on hand (see Figure 3.4). The potentially constrained repair order is allocated between government depot and commercial overhaul according to capacity levels at each location. The overhaul rates may be limited by production capacity levels. As inventory is repaired, it is shipped to serviceable inventory available for issue.

Once orders are placed for overhaul and new production, orders are then placed with the first-tier suppliers for the components necessary to assemble the final product. Figure 3.5 illustrates the model structure for commercial overhaul. Similar structures exist for depot overhaul and new spare production. It is important to note that the overhaul process can begin only if necessary components parts are on hand.

The orders that originate in Figure 3.5 at the OEM or overhaul sites flow to the first-tier suppliers. These suppliers then place orders with the second-tier suppliers, who in turn place orders with the third-tier suppliers as shown in Figure 3.6. Second-tier production can begin only if there is inventory available from the first tier, such as the raw material. In a similar manner, production at the first tier can begin only if there is inventory of output from the second tier. Each tier is dependent on the previous one to complete the process, and each level may be limited by a PLT of another supplier.

As the components are shipped to new production, commercial overhaul, or government depot overhaul, they flow into inventories at these sites. The total availability of components at these locations is determined by the minimum inventory level (see Figure 3.7). This availability value then becomes a factor in the determination of the production and overhaul start rates, seen in Figures 3.3 and 3.5.

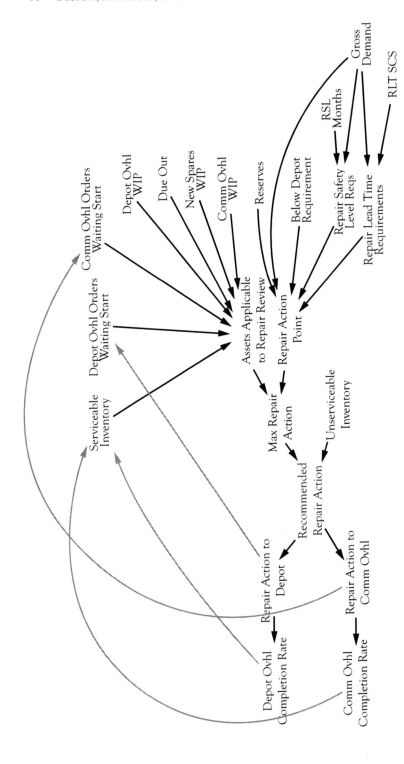

Figure 3.4. Recommended repair actions.

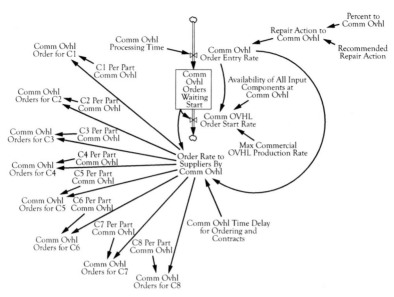

Figure 3.5. Order-placement process to supply chain tiers.

Upon completion of orders through the overhaul and procurement processes, the products are shipped to the central inventory site and then to one of four regional inventories. The parts are pulled from these inventories and placed into service on an aircraft. The damaged or worn parts that are removed are returned for repair, less a percentage that are scrapped or not returned by the field. The returned parts enter the unserviceable inventory on hand and then enter the overhaul process.

Analysis and Simulation Results

The key objectives of the model are as follows: (a) to assess the performance of the requirements-determination process in the presence of a multichannel, multitier supply chain; (b) to evaluate the likelihood of the bullwhip effect being produced in the supply chain and its impact on lower-tier suppliers; (c) to determine the sensitivity of the supply control to inaccurate data; and (d) to evaluate impacts of real-world production and overhaul capacity constraints. The model described has been parameterized for specific high-value parts and has been used to simulate the behavior and performance of the requirements-determination process

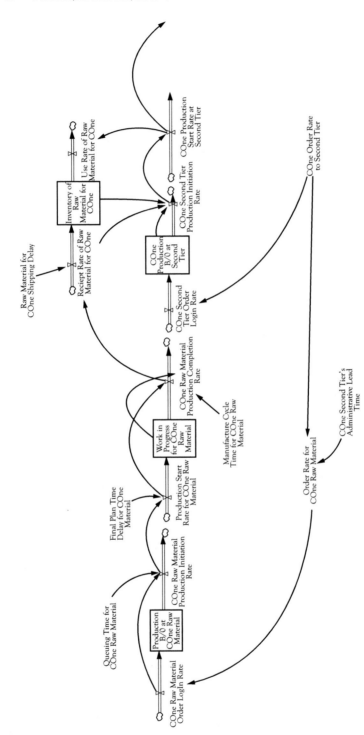

Figure 3.6. Supply chain tiers for component 1.

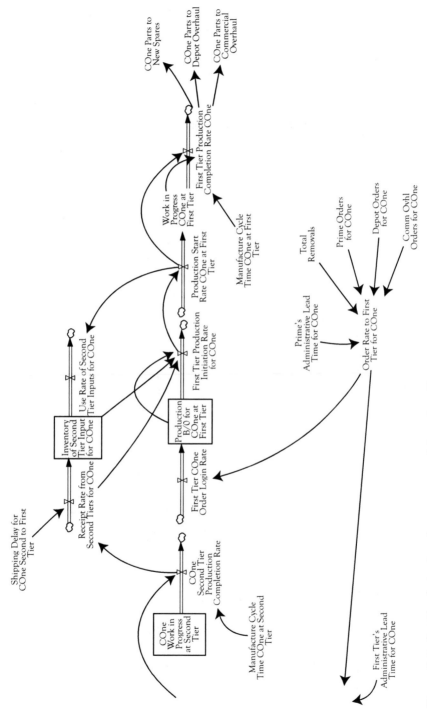

Figure 3.6. Supply chain tiers for component 1 (continued).

and the supply chain for these particular parts. The following cases are presented with a simulation time covering 2001–2012:

Case 1. Constant demand

Case 2. Step-up in demand in 2003

Case 3. Oscillating demand

Case 4. Error in production lead time (PLT) resulting from an increase in PLT at a raw-material supplier; data error persists for one year

Case 5. Production constraint limits production at a first-tier supplier

Cases 1 and 2 were used both in the validation of the model and to verify that the requirements-determination process generated appropriate new procurement and overhaul orders in response to constant demand and a step-up in demand. These two cases also enabled assessment of the behavior of the ordering and production process in the multitier, multi-channel supplier network. Case 3 was conducted to determine whether the governmental computerized-ordering process and the related supply chain exhibited the bullwhip effect and to examine the impacts on the lower-tier suppliers. Because numerous reports have indicated that certain data, such as PLT, used in the ordering process are often incorrect,[6] case 4 investigates the impact of incorrect PLT on the ordering process and supply chain performance. Moreover, because the governmental ordering process does not include the potential for production capacity constraints, case 5 examines the behavior of the supply-control process and the ability of the system to meet rising demand in the presence of capacity constraints. Finally, case 6 examines a "real-world" scenario involving shifting demand, production constraints, and data errors.

Case 1 assumes constant demand of 14 units per month (divided between the four regions—Region A [7 units/month], Region B [5 units/month], Region C [1 unit/month], and Region D [1 unit/month]) as depicted in Figure 3.9. Other key assumptions include no limit on production or overhaul rates, an overall PLT of 22 months, and a repair lead time (RLT) of 11 months. The overall PLT is calculated as the maximum lead time of the eight components plus the PLT and administrative lead time at the primary supplier. The lead time of each component (i.e., of each

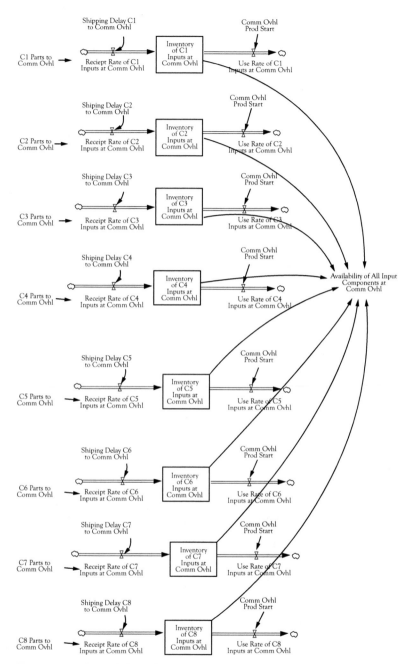

Figure 3.7. Availability of components for assembly.

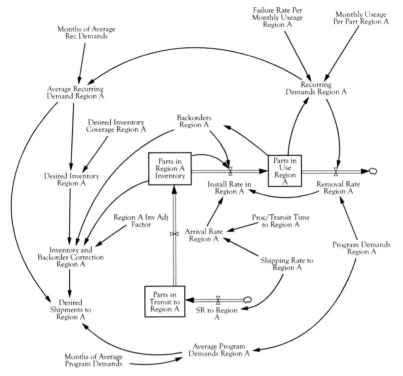

Figure 3.8. Region A demands and returns.

channel) is determined to be the sum of the shipping delays, the manufacture lead times, and the administrative lead times for each tier. The first four cases assume that four components are used for new spare production only and have a common overall lead time of 12.2 months. The other four components are used for both overhaul and new spare production and have a common overall lead time of 8.2 months. For new spare production, the OEM requires 9.8 months for assembly and integration, resulting in the 22-month overall PLT used in the requirements-determination process. For overhaul, the depot and commercial overhaul facility require 2.8 months for integration and assembly, yielding the 11-month overall RLT used in the requirements-determination process. The assumed PLT and RLT for the ordering-determination process are equivalent to the overall actual values in this case.

The simulation output from case 1 is presented in Figures 3.9 to 3.15. Figure 3.9 shows the constant input demands. Figure 3.10 shows that

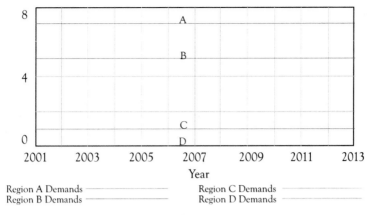

Figure 3.9. Constant demand levels.

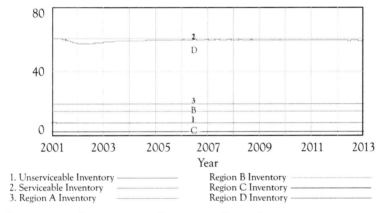

Figure 3.10. Inventories with constant demand.

the central and regional inventory levels remain constant. Figure 3.11 shows that removals, shipments to regional inventories, and production and overhaul rates are constant. The system establishes an equilibrium that is maintained throughout the simulation. Figure 3.12 presents the availability of component inventory at the OEM and the two overhaul sites. The somewhat surprising oscillation in the available components at prime stems from the procurement process. Figure 3.13 shows that when the total net assets dip below the procurement reorder point, a procurement action occurs for a period of time. The procurement action ceases because the procurement action leads to orders that create due-ins increasing total net assets. Once a procurement action is initiated, an

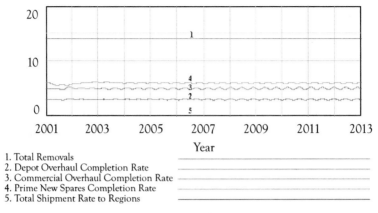

1. Total Removals
2. Depot Overhaul Completion Rate
3. Commercial Overhaul Completion Rate
4. Prime New Spares Completion Rate
5. Total Shipment Rate to Regions

Figure 3.11. Key rates with constant demand.

Availability of Components with Constant Demand

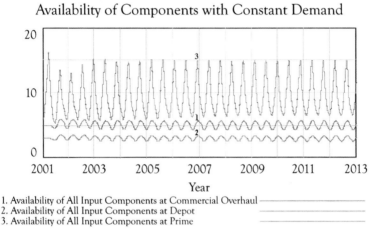

1. Availability of All Input Components at Commercial Overhaul
2. Availability of All Input Components at Depot
3. Availability of All Input Components at Prime

Figure 3.12. Availability of components for the overhaul and production processes with constant demand.

order to the supply chain tiers follows as shown in Figure 3.14. Figure 3.15 shows how these pulsing orders thus create highly variable input inventory at the OEMs even in the face of constant demands. The repair process is more stable because repair actions are limited by the requirement for damaged or worn parts that maintain a constant flow due to constant removals. This stability is shown in Figure 3.14.

Case 2 assumes a step increase in demand from 14 to 18 parts per month in 2003 (each region increasing demand by 1 unit per month), while holding all other assumptions the same as the steady state case. This

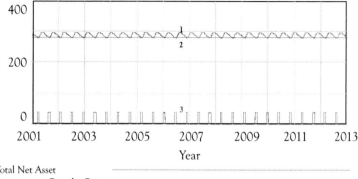

1. Total Net Asset
2. Procurement Reorder Point
3. Procurement Action

Figure 3.13. Procurement action with constant demand.

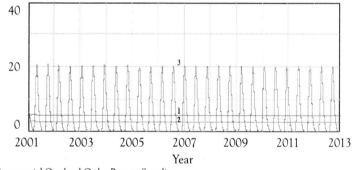

1. Commercial Overhaul Order Rate to Suppliers
2. Depot Overhaul Order Rate to Suppliers
3. Prime Order Rate to Suppliers

Figure 3.14. Order rate of components for overhaul and procurement processes with constant demand.

case illustrates the typical growth in demand that has been seen for aviation parts within the past 5 years and also provides a basic determination of the recovery time of the system after a disturbance from equilibrium.[7] Figure 3.16 illustrates the input demands, and Figure 3.17 presents the serious impacts on the central and regional inventories. As may be seen, the central inventory is depleted for a period of nearly 2 years. This shortage occurs because of the long lead times in production and overhaul of high-value aviation spare parts. As may be seen in Figure 3.18, the new production rate increases in response to the higher demands, but overhaul rates are constrained by the number of unserviceable items on

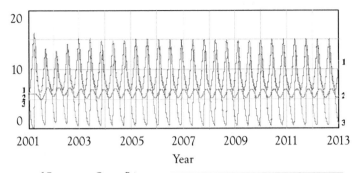

1. Inventory of Component One at Prime
2. Receipt Rate of Component One at Prime
3. Use Rate of Component One at Prime

Figure 3.15. Inventory of component 1 at OEM with constant demand.

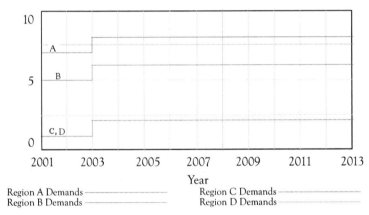

Region A Demands
Region B Demands
Region C Demands
Region D Demands

Figure 3.16. Demand steps up in 2003.

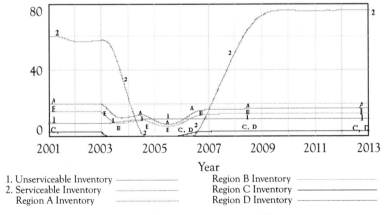

1. Unserviceable Inventory
2. Serviceable Inventory
   Region A Inventory
Region B Inventory
Region C Inventory
Region D Inventory

Figure 3.17. Inventories with a step increase in demand.

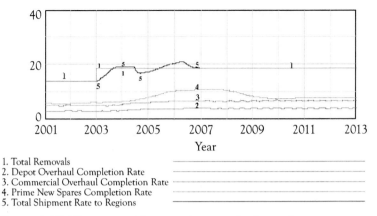

1. Total Removals
2. Depot Overhaul Completion Rate
3. Commercial Overhaul Completion Rate
4. Prime New Spares Completion Rate
5. Total Shipment Rate to Regions

Figure 3.18. Key rates with a step increase in demand.

hand. Component availability presented in Figure 3.19 slowly grows to support higher levels of procurement and overhaul but does not grow fast enough to enable production to halt the depletion of inventory. Since the procurement reorder point is largely determined by a 24-month average demand, the procurement process does not respond to the higher demand for at least a year. As may be seen in Figures 3.20 and 3.21, as the reorder point begins to increase in 2004 and 2005, it causes larger and more frequent orders for new spares. Since raw material is ordered last but used first in the supply chain, the increase in orders causes the raw-material inventory at tier 2 to be quickly depleted and remain at very low levels (see Figure 3.22). The repair process is once again limited

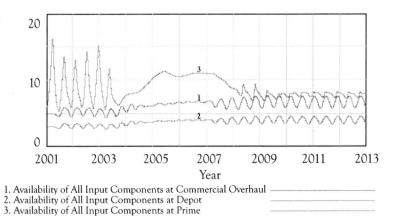

1. Availability of All Input Components at Commercial Overhaul
2. Availability of All Input Components at Depot
3. Availability of All Input Components at Prime

Figure 3.19. Availability of components for the overhaul and production processes with a step increase in demand.

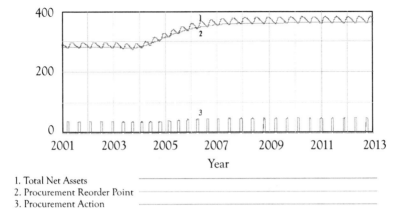

1. Total Net Assets
2. Procurement Reorder Point
3. Procurement Action

Figure 3.20. Procurement action with a step increase in demand.

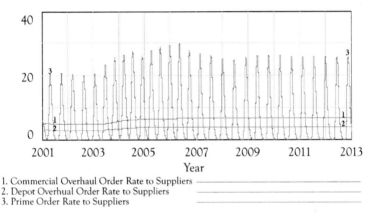

1. Commercial Overhaul Order Rate to Suppliers
2. Depot Overhual Order Rate to Suppliers
3. Prime Order Rate to Suppliers

Figure 3.21. Order rate of components for overhaul and procurement processes with a step increase in demand.

by the unserviceable inventory on hand, as depicted in Figure 3.23, in which the repair action is equal to the unserviceable inventory, while the desired maximum repair is significantly higher. This constraint on the repair action therefore dampens the number of components utilized in overhaul and keeps this process relatively stable.

To examine the potential for the bullwhip effect in this extended supply chain, case 3 assumes a ±20% sinusoidal oscillation in demand over a 4-year period. All other key assumptions from case 1 remain the same. Figure 3.24 presents the input-demand assumptions, and Figure 3.25 shows the considerable variation in inventories. The production and

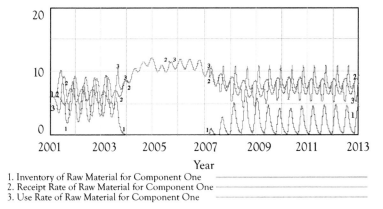

1. Inventory of Raw Material for Component One
2. Receipt Rate of Raw Material for Component One
3. Use Rate of Raw Material for Component One

Figure 3.22. Inventory of raw material for component 1 used in overhaul and procurement processes with a step increase in demand.

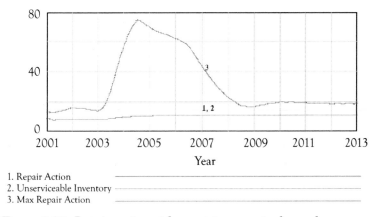

1. Repair Action
2. Unserviceable Inventory
3. Max Repair Action

Figure 3.23. Repair action with a step increase in demand.

overhaul rates fluctuate, but the bullwhip is not severe. This is because of the sequential nature of the ordering process, which does not include amplification but simply passing orders along the chain, and because overhaul variation is limited by unserviceable inventory on hand (see Figure 3.26). Availability of components is also affected by these fluctuations in demands, producing spikes in inventory levels that vary from the initial inventory level by as much as 90% (see Figure 3.27). This volatility is a result of the irregular procurement action, shown in Figure 3.28, which then causes the order rate of components to suppliers to fluctuate (see Figure 3.29). The order rate to suppliers also affects the inventory of

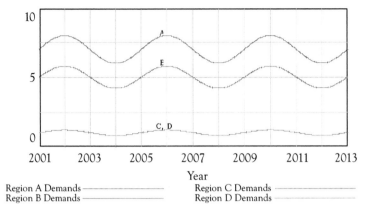

Region A Demands
Region B Demands
Region C Demands
Region D Demands

Figure 3.24. Demand with a 20% oscillation, 4-year oscillation period.

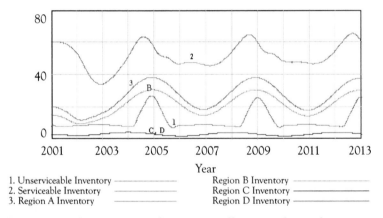

1. Unserviceable Inventory
2. Serviceable Inventory
3. Region A Inventory
Region B Inventory
Region C Inventory
Region D Inventory

Figure 3.25. Inventories with a 20% oscillation in demand, 4-year oscillation period.

materials in the supply chain tiers. Since the raw-material supplier is the last to receive the order, this supplier is affected the most by the instability of the orders, causing the inventory levels at the second tier to suffer. The raw material inventory at the second tier shows significant fluctuations ranging by as much as 100% of the initial inventory levels (see Figure 3.30). Meanwhile, tiers closer to the customer are able to maintain some level of inventory at all times, but this level is still extremely unstable, varying again by about 100% for some short durations (see Figure 3.31). This volatility is also present in the repair process, although the extent of the variation in inventory levels is limited by the unserviceable

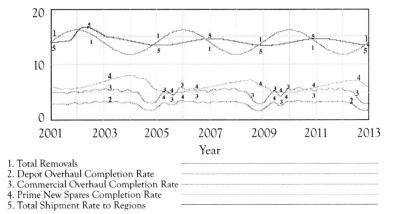

1. Total Removals
2. Depot Overhaul Completion Rate
3. Commercial Overhaul Completion Rate
4. Prime New Spares Completion Rate
5. Total Shipment Rate to Regions

Figure 3.26. Key rates with a 20% oscillation in demand, 4-year oscillation period.

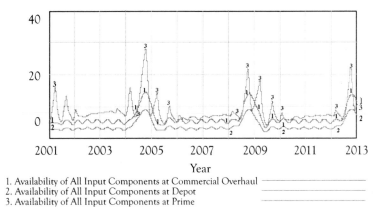

1. Availability of All Input Components at Commercial Overhaul
2. Availability of All Input Components at Depot
3. Availability of All Input Components at Prime

Figure 3.27. Availability of components for the overhaul and production processes with a 20% oscillation in demand and a 4-year oscillation period.

inventory on hand. In this case, however, the repair action is affected by both the limited unserviceable inventory at times and the recommended repair action at other times (see Figure 3.32). The bullwhip effect is therefore still quite evident in the supply chain tiers, as indicated in the component-inventory levels at commercial overhaul in Figure 3.33.

This is all assuming alternative periods for the oscillation in demand greatly affects the supply chain performance (see Figure 3.34). Increasing the period from 2 years to 4 years to 8 years amplifies the bullwhip effect in serviceable inventory, as shown in Figure 3.35.

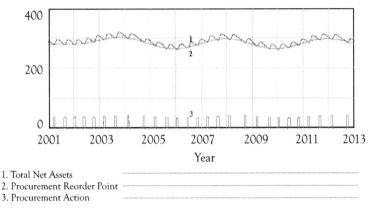

Figure 3.28. Procurement action with a 20% oscillation in demand, 4-year oscillation period.

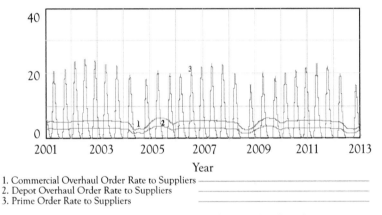

Figure 3.29. Order rate of components for overhaul and procurement processes with a 20% oscillation in demand and a 4-year oscillation period.

A series of simulations was conducted to develop a comparison of the extent of the bullwhip effect's impact on inventory levels, both at the prime supplier and at the third-tier raw-material supplier. The impacts of two variables were examined: the period of the oscillation in demands and the averaging time used to calculate expected demands to reflect future orders (see Table 3.1). The bullwhip effect is clearly evident from the degree of the error in inventory on hand between the constant case

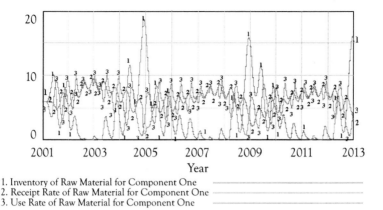

1. Inventory of Raw Material for Component One
2. Receipt Rate of Raw Material for Component One
3. Use Rate of Raw Material for Component One

Figure 3.30. Inventory of raw material component 1 used in overhaul and procurement processes with a 20% oscillation in demand and a 4-year oscillation period.

Inventory of Component One at Prime

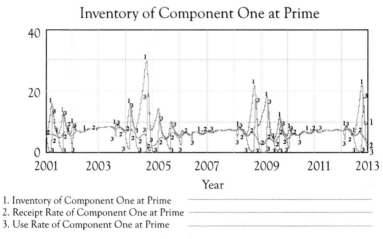

1. Inventory of Component One at Prime
2. Receipt Rate of Component One at Prime
3. Use Rate of Component One at Prime

Figure 3.31. Inventory of material used in procurement process with a 20% oscillation in demand and a 4-year oscillation period.

and the oscillating demand case in the raw-material tier. The amount of the error in serviceable inventory levels between these two cases is dependent on the months of average demand. The government standard of 24 months is most volatile with the longer oscillation periods.

Case 4 examines a problem that frequently occurs in government supply chains for high-value aviation spare parts. This is an error in assumed PLT. In case 4, demand begins at the constant level of 14 parts per month.

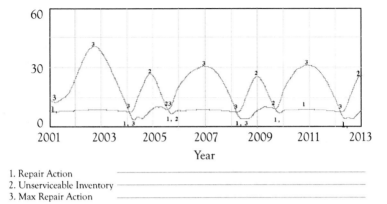

1. Repair Action
2. Unserviceable Inventory
3. Max Repair Action

Figure 3.32. Repair action with a 20% oscillation in demand and a 4-year oscillation period.

Inventory of Component Eight at Commercial Overhaul

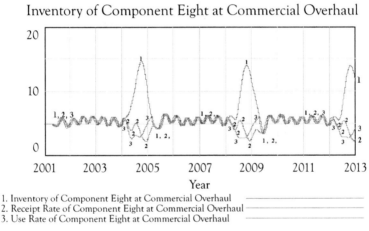

1. Inventory of Component Eight at Commercial Overhaul
2. Receipt Rate of Component Eight at Commercial Overhaul
3. Use Rate of Component Eight at Commercial Overhaul

Figure 3.33. Inventory of material used in overhaul process with a 20% oscillation in demand and a 4-year oscillation period.

In 2003, demand ramps up over 6 months to 18 parts a month, increasing 1 unit per month in each of the four regions. It is then assumed that demand ramps down to the original level over a 2-year period beginning in mid-2009. At the beginning of the simulation, the actual and assumed PLT are both equal to 22 months; in 2004, however, the queuing time for the component 8 raw material increases by 10 months, from 2 to 12 months. Component 8 is a necessary component for both new production and the overhaul process. This assumption reflects circumstances

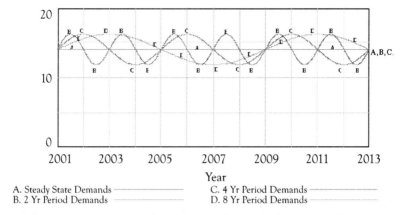

A. Steady State Demands ....   C. 4 Yr Period Demands ....
B. 2 Yr Period Demands ....   D. 8 Yr Period Demands ....

Figure 3.34. Demand with a 20% oscillation and 2-, 4-, and 8-year periods.

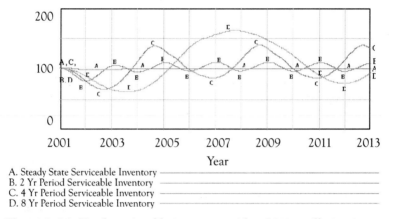

A. Steady State Serviceable Inventory ....
B. 2 Yr Period Serviceable Inventory ....
C. 4 Yr Period Serviceable Inventory ....
D. 8 Yr Period Serviceable Inventory ....

Figure 3.35. Total serviceable inventory with a 20% oscillation in demand and 2-, 4-, and 8-year periods.

that occurred in 2004 as lead times for raw materials increased dramatically. In the case 4 simulation, the assumed PLT remains at 22 months and RLT at 11 months for a year before these values are adjusted in the requirements-determination process to the actual overall values of 32 months and 21 months, respectively. As a result of this error in the calculations for recommended new buys and for overhaul, inventory levels drop for more than 3 years, creating a significant problem within the supply chain process (see Figure 3.36). Because of the error, the control system is assuming that it will receive deliveries much more rapidly than

Table 3.1. Results of Sensitivity Analysis Varying the Period of Demand Oscillation and the Months of Averaging Demand

NO PRODUCTION CONSTRAINTS				
	20% variance in demand	Months of Avg Demand		
	Period	6	12	24
Percent error in Service-able Inventory between constant case and variable demand case	2	23%	23%	17%
	4	53%	43%	40%
	6	52%	48%	52%
	8	42%	48%	57%
	10	37%	47%	57%
Percent error in Raw Mate-rial Inventory between constant case and variable demand case	2	100%	100%	79%
	4	100%	100%	100%
	6	100%	100%	100%
	8	100%	100%	100%
	10	100%	100%	100%

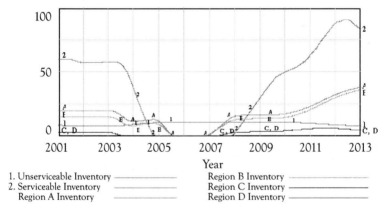

1. Unserviceable Inventory
2. Serviceable Inventory
   Region A Inventory
Region B Inventory
Region C Inventory
Region D Inventory

Figure 3.36. Inventories with a 22–32-month discrepancy in assumed and actual PLT that lasts for 1 year.

it will. In other words, the requirements determination is ordering too little, too late because of this error. This is reflected in the very slowly growing prime new spares completion rate in Figure 3.37. The recommended procurement action is shown in Figure 3.38. An interesting dynamic occurs here. The reorder point begins to rise, thus generating orders and a growing total net assets. However, when the PLT error is

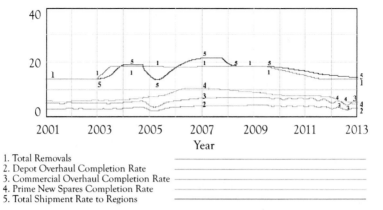

1. Total Removals
2. Depot Overhaul Completion Rate
3. Commercial Overhaul Completion Rate
4. Prime New Spares Completion Rate
5. Total Shipment Rate to Regions

Figure 3.37. Key rates with a 22–32-month discrepancy in assumed and actual PLT that lasts for 1 year.

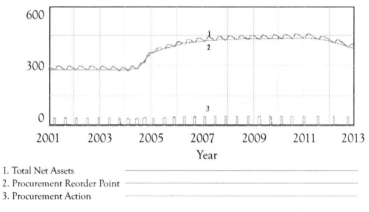

1. Total Net Assets
2. Procurement Reorder Point
3. Procurement Action

Figure 3.38. Procurement action with a 22–32-month discrepancy in assumed and actual PLT that lasts for 1 year.

corrected during 2005, it causes the reorder point to increase and effectively reduce the gap between itself and the total net assets. The result is a counterintuitive reduction in the recommended orders (see Figure 3.39). This prolongs the problems with available inventory. Although the recommended repair action reflects the same increase as the production order rate, overhaul is once again limited by the amount of unserviceable inventory on hand (see Figure 3.40), and repair actions are much less than the desired maximum repair action.

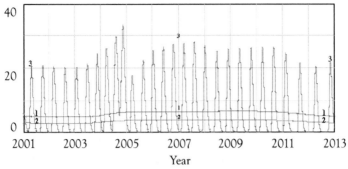

1. Commercial Overhaul Order Rate to Suppliers
2. Depot Overhaul Order Rate to Suppliers
3. Prime Order Rate to Suppliers

Figure 3.39. Order rate of components for overhaul and procurement processes with a 22–32-month discrepancy in assumed and actual PLT for 1 year.

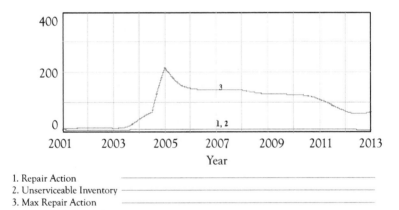

1. Repair Action
2. Unserviceable Inventory
3. Max Repair Action

Figure 3.40. Repair action with a 22–32-month discrepancy in assumed and actual PLT that lasts for 1 year.

Figures 3.41 and 3.42 show the sensitivity of the supply chain to changes in the queuing time for raw material. The effects on serviceable inventory levels are notable. In particular, the last case, in which the PLT increases by 9 months, causes almost a year's delay in the start of the recovery of the inventory levels in comparison to the case in which there is no error. In a similar manner and to a much greater extent, these delays affect the raw-material inventory levels at tier 2. As may be seen in Figure 3.42, as would be expected, the greater the PLT and the error, the

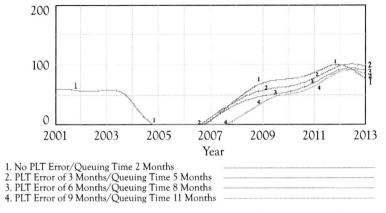

1. No PLT Error/Queuing Time 2 Months
2. PLT Error of 3 Months/Queuing Time 5 Months
3. PLT Error of 6 Months/Queuing Time 8 Months
4. PLT Error of 9 Months/Queuing Time 11 Months

Figure 3.41. Serviceable inventory with varying errors in PLT lasting for 1 year.

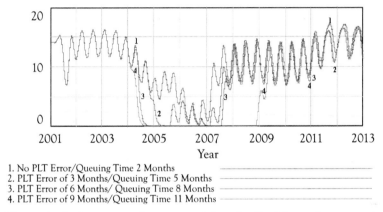

1. No PLT Error/Queuing Time 2 Months
2. PLT Error of 3 Months/Queuing Time 5 Months
3. PLT Error of 6 Months/ Queuing Time 8 Months
4. PLT Error of 9 Months/Queuing Time 11 Months

Figure 3.42. Inventory of raw material at tier 2 with varying errors in PLT lasting for 1 year.

longer the duration of depleted inventory levels. During this time, back orders are growing at the tier 3 raw-material supplier, and inventory levels throughout the supply chain are greatly affected.

Case 5 examines another "real-world" scenario that occurs frequently and involves production constraints. Production limitations or constraints are not included in the algorithms of the requirements-determination process used by many government agencies. In reality, however, availability of tooling and labor does limit these processes. Case 5 assumes a ramp-up in demand in 2003 from 14 to 18 parts per month and a ramp-down in demand beginning in 2009 to 14 parts per month. All other assumptions from case 1 remain the same, except, however, component 8, which is necessary for both overhaul and procurement processes and has a production constraint at the first tier of 20 parts per month. Without this constraint, the first-tier supplier of this component should generally be producing up to 22 parts per month after the ramp-up in demand. Limiting this production by this small difference delays the start of the recovery of serviceable inventory by about 9 months, from late 2006 to mid-2007 (see Figure 3.43). In addition, the inventory levels do not fully recover nearly as quickly as the case in which there are no production constraints (see case 4), and therefore do not reach the level necessary to sustain the higher demand levels before demand ramps back down.

Figure 3.44 presents the results of a sensitivity analysis of the impacts of varying the production limit on component 8 at tier 1. In the unconstrained case, production is roughly 22 units per month. Reducing the limitation to 20 or 21 components per month has a significant impact on the recovery of serviceable inventory. At a limit of 19 components per month, the serviceable inventory levels do not begin to recover for approximately 4 years after the unconstrained simulation. Both case 4, incorporating the impacts of inaccurate data, and case 5, assuming production constraints, demonstrate the high sensitivity of this extended supply chain and the high risk of performance problems. Many government supply chains balance on this knife edge where small changes can create major problems.

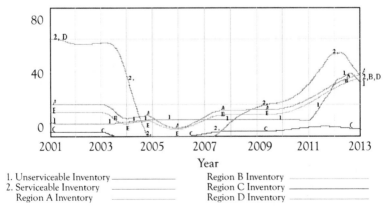

Figure 3.43. Inventories with a 20/month production limit on component 8 at tier 1.

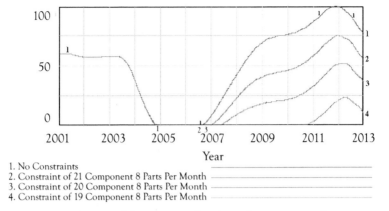

1. No Constraints
2. Constraint of 21 Component 8 Parts Per Month
3. Constraint of 20 Component 8 Parts Per Month
4. Constraint of 19 Component 8 Parts Per Month

Figure 3.44. Serviceable inventory levels with varying production constraints on component 8 at tier 1.

Conclusions

Supply chains for high-value aviation spare parts have experienced considerable problems in assuring stable supply. Many of these problems are shown to be the result of the reordering or requirements-determination process, the high sensitivity to inaccurate data and production constraints, and the extended complexity of the multitier, multichannel supply chains. Three key findings have emerged:

1. The bullwhip effect is strongly evident in the supply chain, causing inventory levels to vary greatly throughout all tiers of the supply chain.
2. Because the ordering process determines recommended procurement and overhaul actions by subtracting two large numbers, the ordering process and the resulting supply chain performance are extremely sensitive to noise and inaccurate data.
3. Because the requirements-determination process does not include the possibility of production constraints, supply chain performance deteriorates rapidly in the face of such constraints.

The system dynamics model successfully revealed the preceding findings and the dangers of misunderstanding the underlying causes of supply chain problems.

CHAPTER 4

Using System Dynamics to Evaluate a Push-Pull Inventory Optimization Strategy for Multitier, Multichannel Supply Chains

Introduction

Demand planning is a harsh reality because of a simple and straightforward fact: *the forecast is always wrong.*[1] Demand forecasting is especially challenging for products such as aviation spare parts with long production lead times (PLTs), unknown future operating environments, and uncertain political developments. This fundamental forecasting and planning requirement has been a problem for the proper management of government supply chains for half a century or longer.[2] Inventory shortages and back orders frequently afflict government supply, although excess inventory has caused unnecessary expenditure as well.[3] The government has had a long-term need for a strategy that would improve its ability to meet unexpected demands while minimizing expenditure. Numerous studies have been performed and suggestions made for meeting these requirements, but to date these issues continue to produce significant impacts that hinder readiness improvements and supply availability within the government supply chain.[4] This chapter presents an approach for an innovative strategy for improving availability of aviation spare parts in an efficient and effective fashion.

Figure 4.1 presents an overview of the extended enterprise supply chain for aviation spare parts. This supply chain extends from raw-material producers through multitier production supply chains to a prime contractor integrator and then on to inventory and aircraft in global regions. In Figure 4.1, 10 components are each produced in a three-tier supply chain and then assembled into the final spare part. A subset of the 10 components is required for depot overhaul, and another subset is required for commercial overhaul. (Parts in need of repair are shipped to overhaul facilities after removal in the field.) New spares and overhauled spares enter a central inventory site and then are distributed to global inventory points based on received orders. Regional demand is driven by the number of aircraft in each region, the monthly flight hours per aircraft in each region, and a failure rate per flight hour in each specific region. As may be seen in Figure 4.1, demand information flows back to the ordering process and is used to calculate future demands and future requirements. The ordering process through which demand information is used to calculate production and overhaul quantities is known as the requirements-determination process and is based on algorithms that date back to the 1960s.[5] In this process, an averaging of historical demand (typically a 24-month rolling average) is used to predict future requirements, and this information, in addition to current due-ins and due-outs, is compared to available inventory levels to determine recommended buys and repairs. As orders for the new buys and repairs are processed

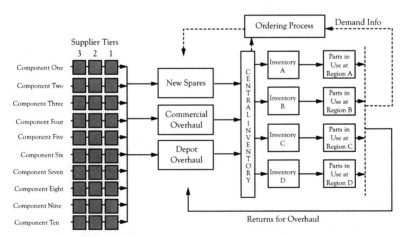

Figure 4.1. Overview of the supply chain for aviation parts.

and ultimately produced, available inventory is affected; thus, a feedback control system is apparent in which the feedback of demand information is central.

One approach that is often chosen to improve forecast accuracy is to apply more historical data to the forecasting calculations.[6] Unfortunately for many organizations, historical data are not available, and when they are, the data are often inaccurate.[7] This is frequently the case for defense-related items such as aviation spare parts. Furthermore, the current ordering process of the government supply chain leaves very little room for data or forecast error. The principal method for calculating recommended buys and repairs is based on determining the difference between two large numbers.[8] As a result, relatively minor standard deviations among the original terms compound to cause significant error in the resulting orders. This can have a highly negative effect on the efficacy of the entire demand planning and ordering process.

Rather than trying to improve the forecasting calculations, Rand Corporation suggests focusing on improving supply chain responsiveness.[9] One straightforward strategy for increased responsiveness is simply to hold a substantial amount of safety stock in a "push" supply approach. The safety-stock inventory levels are predetermined based on anticipated demands. In this tactic, spare parts are "pushed" out to global regional distribution centers awaiting orders from customers. This strategy is shown in Figure 4.2 as line A. This approach, while improving responsiveness, can be extremely costly due to the high cost of holding large regional inventories of finished spare parts.[10] Curve A in Figure 4.3 illustrates the commonly held view between readiness (supply availability) and investment in stocks. As higher levels of readiness are targeted, a much higher level of investment is required. This is illustrated by the rightmost vertical arrow in Figure 4.3. In other words, add money and move up the readiness curve.

Another approach is to introduce a push-pull strategy in the distribution portion of the extended supply chain. In such a strategy, parts with higher monthly demand and lower demand variability are pushed out to the regional inventories since the demand requirements are fairly well known. On the other hand, parts with low monthly demand and high demand variability tend to be held in the central inventory. This

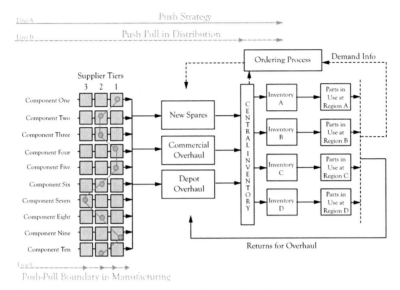

Figure 4.2. Push strategy compared to push-pull strategy.

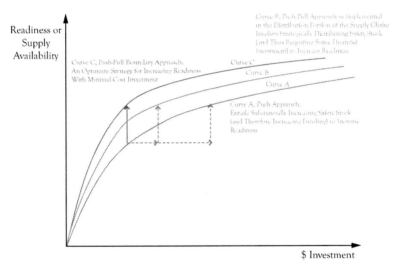

Figure 4.3. Supply strategies relative to cost.

aggregates demand volatility across the regions and holds stock that can then be sent where needed, thus reducing costs. This approach is shown as line B in Figure 4.2. Improvement in readiness is no longer achieved by moving from point to point on line A; the optimization strategy creates a completely new relationship curve between readiness and investment. On line B, it requires a much smaller investment to achieve the targeted readiness. This is illustrated by the middle vertical arrow on Figure 4.3.

Yet another strategy is to create a "push-pull" boundary within the multitier, multichannel manufacturing supply chain.[11] The location of the boundary depends on the committed service time (CST) of the final product and the variability of demand. In this circumstance, inventories of certain work-in-progress (WIP) items are created (i.e., pushed forward) in the manufacturing supply chain. These WIP inventories are then available to be used in the manufacturing process depending on the pull of customer demand. For example, certain forgings or castings might be held in inventory to avoid long waits for raw materials and the casting or forging process. It is important to note that these items have relatively low value added since much of the final value is added later through, for example, labor-intensive and capital-intensive precision machining. This holding of lower value-added items contributes to the cost savings of this approach.

Determining the appropriate inventory levels within the manufacturing supply chain requires conducting a trade-off analysis between the holding cost of the inventory, the value added along the tiers, the production time at each tier, average demand levels, variability of demand, and required customer service time. In general, the shorter the required customer service time, the larger the inventory needed and the closer to the final product. If longer service times are acceptable, then inventories can be smaller and placed further back in the supply chain—that is, in the lower tiers of the manufacturing supply chain. This analysis can be structured as an optimization problem solving for the lowest cost given required customer service time, demand levels, demand variability, manufacturing times, and value added within the channels of the supply chain network. The solution determines the optimal level of WIP safety stock for each supplier in the supply chain, creating a boundary between the push and pull systems. This strategy creates yet another relationship between readiness and investment in which very little additional investment is required to achieve the targeted readiness. This is achieved by optimally holding lower value-added inventory to enable responsiveness.

Optimization Approach

The importance of using optimization software tools for inventory management in the government sector was emphasized in a *Jane's Defense Weekly* article almost a decade ago.[12] Despite this early analysis, even recent Government Accountability Office (GAO) reports have indicated the need for continued analysis of safety stock levels.[13] In addition, Rand Corporation has conducted research into government supply chains and has noted that increased inventory management would benefit readiness capabilities.[14] Inventory-management policies, including maintaining key amounts of safety stock throughout the supply chain, create a balance of push and pull supply chain strategies, an approach that, according to David Simchi-Levi, may be ideal.[15] Villa and Watanabe conducted a detailed analysis of this push-pull combination more than a decade ago.[16] More recently, a number of researchers have analyzed push-pull strategies and optimization techniques and their effect on commercial and government supply chains. Minnich and Maier have thoroughly discussed the benefits and drawbacks of push and pull strategies.[17] Rand has suggested applying push-pull supply chain techniques to the government supply chain.[18] Chandra and Grabis discuss inventory management and its effect on lead time and cost.[19] Lan, Chu, Chung, Wan, and Lo address optimization of order quantities and lead times,[20] and Simchi-Levi and Zhao discuss safety stock optimization in supply chains with varying lead times.[21] Lee, Chew, Teng, and Chen apply optimization techniques to aircraft parts allocation.[22] Killingsworth, Chavez, and Martin conduct a thorough analysis of the government supply chain through the application of high-value aviation spare parts in a multichannel, multiechelon system dynamics supply chain model that embeds the government ordering process.[23] The intent of the current research is to apply optimization techniques to the inventory management of the government supply chain for a high-value aviation part. The approach uses a commercial software package that establishes a balance of push and pull and thus helps to increase readiness, limit stock-outs, and shorten recoverability from increased changes in demand.

It must be noted that the optimization process is a steady state or static solution. That is, it determines optimum WIP inventory given a specific constant average demand level (i.e., mean demand), constant demand variability (i.e., standard deviation of demand), and a committed customer-service time. If a different average demand is assumed, then a different optimal solution is calculated, as would be expected. It is important, therefore, to understand and evaluate likely supply chain performance given optimum WIP inventories but time-varying demand scenarios such as a sharp surge in demand. To test and evaluate the optimum solutions, a dynamic simulation model has been developed of the multitier, multichannel extended enterprise supply system illustrated in Figures 4.1 and 4.2. This model simulates the behavior and performance of the extended supply chain for alternative assumptions of WIP inventory and time-varying demands. Optimum WIP inventories, for example, are established in the manufacturing supply chain, and part availability over time is evaluated and measured via simulations with alternative demand scenarios.

Description of the Optimization Process

The software used for the current research is Inventory Analyst, a commercial inventory optimization software package developed and distributed by LogicTools, a division of ILOG. Inventory Analyst is widely used by major corporations for supply chain design and optimization. Users include such supply chain leaders as Colgate-Palmolive Company, ConAgra Foods, and Kraft.

Inventory Analyst requires as input a basic map of the supply chain being analyzed. Figure 4.4 shows the supply chain map for the part being analyzed in this pilot study, a helicopter main rotor blade that consists of 10 key, long-lead-time parts. This map shows the supply network for the production of the new helicopter blade. The overall supply chain is composed of numerous suppliers, each of which ultimately produces a component that is then integrated into a final assembly process at the OEM. The diagram also includes the estimated PLT (in days) of each of the manufacturing processes. Also indicated are the number of each component part that is needed in the final assembly. The first nine components are considered critical items in that they have the longest lead times. They are therefore principal determinants of the lengthy delay in the ordering process for this aviation part. Component 10 is a "catch-all" bin for the remaining items that compose the final product.

Figure 4.5 presents a similar map for the necessary parts required for the overhaul of a blade.

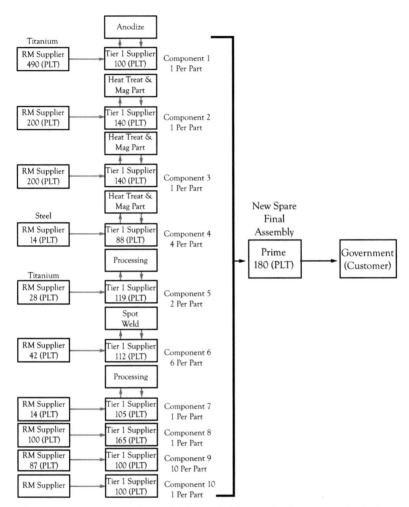

Figure 4.4. Overview of a multitier, multichannel aviation supply chain.

Figure 4.6 shows an expanded and integrated view of the flows present in Figures 4.4 and 4.5 and in the model. For this particular part, all
overhaul is conducted commercially; there is no depot overhaul. As seen
in Figure 4.5, overhaul requires only 3 of the 10 components, while new
production requires all the components to produce the final product. The
map in Figure 4.6 shows the safety stock placement opportunities. For
example, raw material may be held at the raw-material supplier or at the
tier 1 supplier. In a similar manner, a component may be stored at its

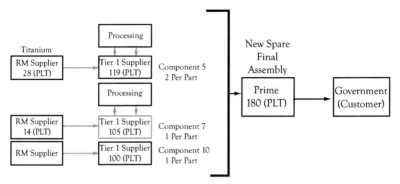

Figure 4.5. Overview of the aviation repair process.

originating supplier or at the subsequent assembly location. Each of these possibilities is taken into consideration in the optimization process.

In the optimization model, demand originates in the government sector, which is defined as a consumption-based customer. Overall demand is assumed to be 22 blades per month. The loss and scrap rate for the blades in the field is assumed to be 6%; that is, only 94% of the removed blades are returned to be evaluated for overhaul. The scrap rate at the overhaul facility is assumed to be 46%. Thus for 22 blades being removed each month, 11 end up being available for overhaul [22 × (1 - 0.06) × (1 - 0.46)]. The remaining demand must therefore be met with production of new blades. There is thus, in summary, a monthly demand for 11 new blades and 11 overhauled blades. Each of the necessary components is then ordered depending on the number needed for each new part and each overhauled part. Some components are needed in higher quantities to create a final product, while only one of other components is needed to complete a part. Figure 4.4 provides details on the required number of components per part. Each component, furthermore, has a separate lead time for each step of the supply chain process. Therefore the total lead time for the component with the longest lead time plus the final assembly time at the OEM is the overall total PLT for the final product. It is important to note that the PLT for the OEM is 180 days. Thus it takes 6 months to assemble the final product after all the components have been received. This production time is very long and is a major factor in the optimization for required inventories and associated costs. Impacts of reducing this PLT are studied in the optimization calculations. The repair lead time (RLT) is similarly a very

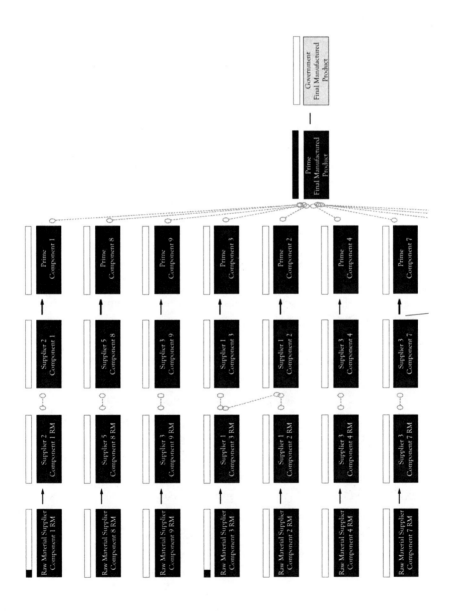

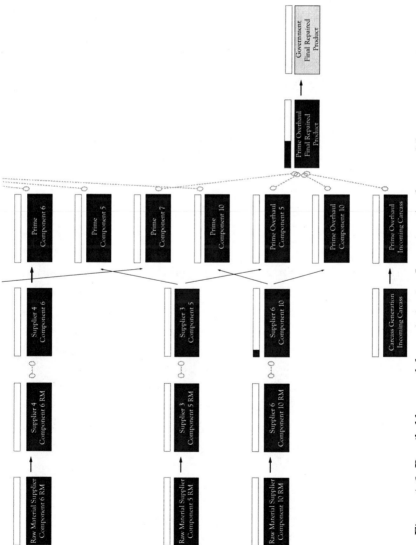

Figure 4.6. Detailed layout of the optimization Inventory Analyst model.

lengthy process at the OEM. The repair process requires the replacement of designated components (two of which in this case are considered critical items) and completion of the final assembly. The impacts of reducing this RLT are also studied in the optimization calculations.

The optimization model also incorporates the cost of each component as well as the cost of the final product. In this case, the overall cost of the final product is assumed to be $175,000. The OEM pays a total of 50% of that cost for the parts needed to assemble the final product, broken down such that component 10 composes 20% of the OEM's cost; components 1 and 4 each compose 15% of the OEM's cost; components 2, 3, and 8 each compose 10% of the OEM's cost; and components 5, 6, 7, and 9 each compose 5% of the OEM's cost. First-tier suppliers then pay 50% of the OEM's cost for the parts needed to assemble their products. These assumptions approximate proprietary costing data. The holding cost of each component is assumed to be 20% of its value. The model uses these key input assumptions to determine an optimum safety stock level based on specified assumptions in CST, demand level, forecast error (i.e., demand variability), and PLT at the OEM.

Inventory Analyst Cases and Results

Inventory Analyst (IA) optimizes stocking levels within a supply chain to achieve lowest cost in the presence of demand uncertainty and a CST. The optimized solution provides the optimum safety stocking level at each location where stocking is allowed. This solution is based on specific assumptions for parameters such as CST, the response time from the order point of a product to the delivery point; fill rate, the percentage of orders that are filled on time; PLT, the time it takes to manufacture a product; RLT, the time it takes to replace designated components and complete the final assembly process; and WIP, inventory that is still in a production stage prior to being available to meet demand.

In all the cases considered in the following discussion, the average total monthly demand is assumed to be 22, with demand for 11 new spares and 11 overhaul spares as noted earlier. For each major category of case, optimum solutions are presented with CSTs of 30, 90, and 240 days:

> *Case 1.* OEM's PLT is 180 days and RLT is 90 days, and no safety stock is created in the manufacturing tiers (this more or less represents the current situation).

Case 2. OEM's PLT is 180 days and RLT is 90 days, and safety stock in the manufacturing chain is optimized.

Case 3. OEM's PLT is 120 days and RLT is 60 days, and no safety stock is created in the manufacturing tiers.

Case 4. OEM's PLT is 120 days and RLT is 60 days, and safety stock is optimized in the manufacturing chain.

PLT of 180 Days and 90 Days

Tables 4.1 and 4.2 present the Inventory Analyst solutions when OEM PLT is 180 days for new products and 90 days for overhaul products. Table 4.1 provides the optimum solutions when the IA model assumptions are structured to allow no safety stock in the manufacturing tiers. This assumption means that all parts below the OEM level are made to order, and the full PLT for all components is felt by the OEM. This corresponds to the current situation in which there is little to no safety stock inventory in the manufacturing supply chain. The cases in Table 4.1 thus solve for the safety stock that must be held by the OEM to maintain the fill rate and committed service time. Table 4.2 presents the optimum solution in which the IA model assumptions allow for the optimization of safety stock in the manufacturing tiers. Here, suppliers in the manufacturing tiers hold safety stock of components and component raw materials to maintain fill rate to the government under the specific assumptions.

In all cases, a 95% fill rate is assumed; that is, 95% of all orders are filled within the CST. The first column of each table gives the demand uncertainty (as a standard deviation), assuming a mean demand of 11 per month for both new and overhaul products. The tables present the solutions for three different levels of demand uncertainty; the demands for each type of product (new and overhaul) are 11 ± 3, 11 ± 6, and 11 ± 9. The second column presents the four levels of assumed CST. The tables then present the associated working capital tied up in inventory, the safety stock levels for new spares, and overhaul spares. Finally, inventories are also presented for finished component 1 and raw materials for component 1. These inventories are presented because component 1 is the component with the longest PLT and thus illustrates the nature of the optimum solutions.

It is important to note that in these cases, Inventory Analyst has been configured to use the Skellam distribution that has the assumed standard deviation, but no nonzero probability, rather than a standard normal distribution. This selection of an IA capability eliminates the difficulties that may arise from that negative demand associated with a normal distribution. This is important for cases such as these in which the standard deviation is large relative to the mean.

As may be seen in Table 4.1, the calculated safety stock is zero for both component 1 and the raw material for component 1. This is because the IA optimization problem has been structured to disallow the storage of any safety stock in the manufacturing tiers. This forces all safety stock, necessary to maintain fill rate in the face of demand uncertainty, to reside in (expensive) finished parts at the OEM plant. As the CST decreases, the necessary safety stock of finished products increases, thus increasing working capital substantially. For example, a demand uncertainty of 3 requires a new spares safety stock of 3.1, making working capital approximately $24 million. On the other hand, a demand uncertainty of 9 combined with a CST of 30 requires 102 new spares in safety

Table 4.1. Solutions with No Stocking in the Manufacturing Tiers

Demand uncertainty	CST (days)	Working capital ($)	New spares safety stock	Overhaul safety stock	Safety stock of finished component 1	Safety stock of component 1 raw material
3	30	31,075,380	29.7	16.6	0	0
	90	30,543,770	28.5	14.3	0	0
	240	27,729,530	23.9	0	0	0
	770	24,075,310	3.1	0	0	0
6	30	40,028,020	64.7	36.6	0	0
	90	38,760,630	62.5	30.3	0	0
	240	33,003,230	53.9	0	0	0
	770	24,778,470	7.1	0	0	0
9	30	49,192,260	102	55.6	0	0
	90	46,977,490	96.5	46.3	0	0
	240	38,276,930	83.9	0	0	0
	770	25,481,630	11.1	0	0	0

All times are in days. OEM PLT is 180 days for new products and 90 days for overhaul products.

stock, making working capital over \$49 million. Also note that Table 4.1 includes the case in which the CST is 770 days. This timeframe is approximately equivalent to the time required to produce an end item starting from its raw material. Very little safety stock is held, and as a result the delivery time from order placement to order fulfillment is reprehensibly long. This situation exemplifies the current inventory policy and provides a basis for the long lead times typical in the aviation industry.

In Table 4.2, the manufacturing safety stock is no longer zero; IA optimizes the safety stock levels at all locations. Notice the substantial reduction in working capital as compared to Table 4.1, particularly for the high-demand uncertainty cases. Note that in Table 4.1, for the 30-day CST with demand uncertainty 9, 102 new products must be stored at the OEM if no safety stock is allowed in the manufacturing tiers, but, as seen in Table 4.2, only 41.1 are recommended if manufacturing safety stock is allowed. The much less expensive manufacturing safety stock is sufficient to maintain fill rate at a much lower level of working capital.

Figure 4.7 corresponds to the solution in Table 4.2 for a demand uncertainty of 3 and a CST of 240 days. The expanded section shows the

Table 4.2. Solutions with Stocking in the Manufacturing Tiers

Demand uncertainty	CST (days)	Working capital (\$)	New spares safety stock	Overhaul safety stock	Safety stock of finished component 1	Safety stock of component 1 raw material
3	30	29,091,250	11.1	8.5	11.1	24.4
	90	27,173,290	8.8	0.6	11.1	24.4
	240	25,285,860	0.8	0.0	7.5	24.4
6	30	34,577,050	26.8	18.5	22.6	52.4
	90	31,154,050	19.8	1.6	23.1	52.4
	240	26,452,480	0.90	0	16.3	52.4
9	30	40,512,690	41.1	28.5	37.1	81.4
	90	35,271,080	30.8	3.5	36.1	81.4
	240	27,766,950	1.0	0	25.4	81.4

All times are in days. OEM PLT is 180 days for new products and 90 days for overhaul products.

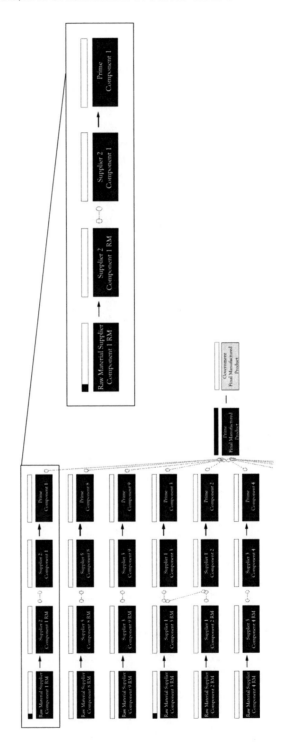

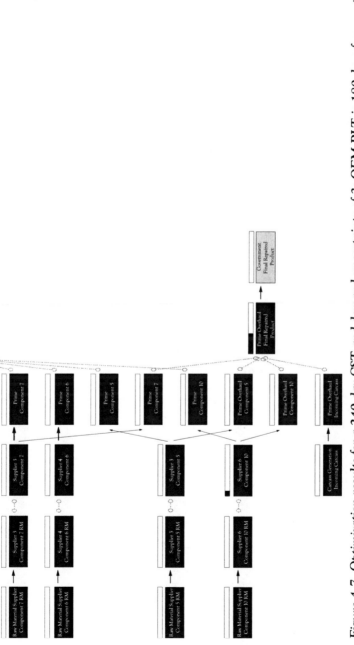

Figure 4.7. Optimization results for a 240-day CST and demand uncertainty of 3; OEM PLT is 180 days for new products and 90 days for overhaul products.

recommended safety stock placement in the component 1 supply chain. Essentially, 24 units of raw material and 7 units of completed component 1 product should be stored at the tier 1 supplier. These stock levels reduce CST without the sacrifice of an extensive budget, as noted in the graph in Figure 4.8.

Figure 4.8 presents a graph of the working capital as a function of CST for the three demand uncertainties of 3, 6, and 9 as presented in Table 4.1 and Table 4.2. Line 1 is the case of no stocking in the manufacturing tiers, and line 2 is the case with stocking in the manufacturing tiers. Note the substantial reductions in cost for low CSTs. Also note that while cost is essentially linear upward from 770 days for the no-stock case, it is nearly flat for the stocking case down to a CST of about 200 days. Given that the current orders take 770 days to be filled, one can immediately cut the CST by nearly a factor of four with virtually no increase in cost, *if* stocking is allowed in the manufacturing tiers.

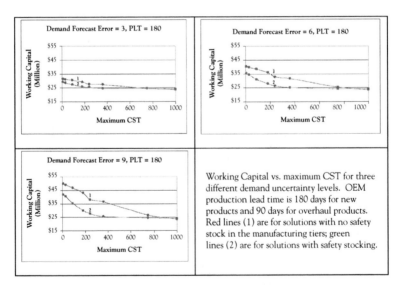

Figure 4.8. Working capital versus maximum CST for three different demand uncertainty levels.

Reduced OEM PLT of 120 Days and 60 Days

An additional strategy for improving availability and reducing working capital is to reduce the PLT at the OEM by, for instance, adopting lean techniques and practices. Table 4.3 and Table 4.4 are identical to Table 4.1 and Table 4.2, respectively, except that Table 4.3 and Table 4.4 are for the OEM PLT of 120 days for new products and 60 days for overhaul products, rather than 180 days and 90 days, respectively. Not surprisingly, the working capital goes down substantially compared to the cases presented in Table 4.1 and Table 4.2 with the same CST values. Much of this capital reduction, about $5 million, arises purely from the reduced holding cost at the final assembly plant due to the lower PLT there. Additional cost savings are realized, however, because the safety stock levels necessary to accommodate demand uncertainty are much lower when the OEM can respond with greater agility. The greatest additional savings are realized for demand uncertainty of 9 and a 30-day CST with stocking in the manufacturing tiers allowed. Here the additional benefit, as compared to the corresponding case presented in Table 4.2, is about $3 million. Comparing the component safety stock levels in Table 4.4 with these entries in Table 4.2, we find little change in the safety stock levels until CST of 240, because the lead times are so long (100 days at tier 1, 490 days at tier 2); however, for the OEM, safety stock levels drop dramatically.

Figure 4.9 illustrates the necessary safety stock levels for the case in which the demand uncertainty is 3 and the CST is 240 days. The optimal safety stock level for component 1 is 24 raw material units at the tier 1 supplier, similar to the case in which the OEM's PLT was 180 days, but, in this case, only 2 completed components need to be stored at this supplier. This difference adds to the working capital savings illustrated in Figure 4.10, as compared to the longer PLT cases.

Figure 4.10 shows the working capital as a function of CST for the three demand uncertainties, 3, 6, and 9. These charts look qualitatively very similar to those in Figure 4.8. Again, the dominant difference is the fixed savings of about $5 million arising purely from reduced holding cost in final assembly. The subtler effect of the savings in safety stock is harder to observe qualitatively, although, from studying the tables, it can be seen that the best additional gain is for a CST of 30 and demand

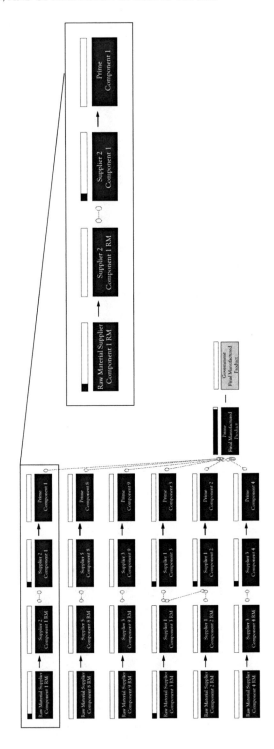

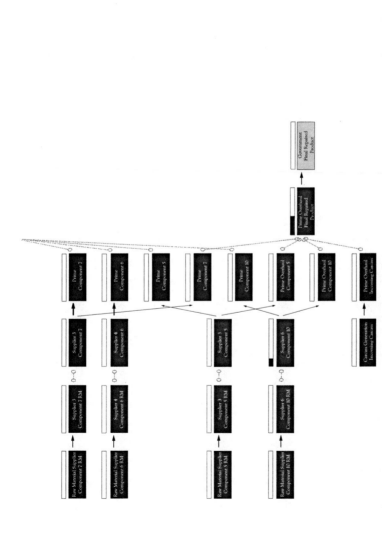

Figure 4.9. Optimization results for a 240-day CST and demand uncertainty of 3; OEM PLT is 120 days for new products and 60 days for overhaul products.

Table 4.3. Solutions with No Stocking in the Manufacturing Tiers

Demand uncertainty	CST (days)	Working capital ($)	New safety stock	Overhaul safety stock	Safety stock of finished component 1	Safety stock of component 1 raw material
3	30	22,498,140	8.8	5.4	11.1	24.4
	90	21,092,450	4.6	1.0	11.1	24.4
	240	19,440,370	0.8	0	2.3	24.4
6	30	27,261,310	19.8	12.4	23.1	52.4
	90	23,951,860	10.6	1.0	23.1	52.4
	240	20,180,590	1.0	0	5.2	52.4
9	30	32,116,350	31.2	19.4	35.8	81.4
	90	27,053,680	17.6	1.0	36.1	81.4
	240	20,912,560	1.0	0	6.2	81.4

All times are in days. OEM PLT is 120 days for new products and 60 days for overhaul products.

Table 4.4. Solutions with Stocking in the Manufacturing Tiers

Demand uncertainty	CST (days)	Working capital ($)	New safety stock	Overhaul safety stock	Safety stock of finished component 1	Safety stock of component 1 raw material
3	30	25,352,210	28.5	15.4	0	0
	90	24,504,810	26.3	12.2	0	0
	240	22,163,160	22.7	0	0	0
6	30	33,849,060	62.5	33.4	0	0
	90	32,265,880	59.3	26.2	0	0
	240	27,085,280	50.7	0	0	0
9	30	42,345,920	96.5	51.4	0	0
	90	40,026,950	92.3	40.2	0	0
	240	32,007,400	78.7	0	0	0

All times are in days. OEM PLT is 120 days for new products and 60 days for overhaul products.

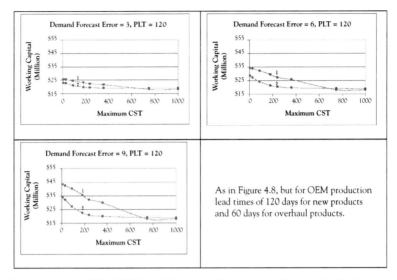

Figure 4.10. OEM PLTs of 120 days for new products and 60 days for overhaul products.

uncertainty of 9; thus, a small change can be noted in the slope at that locus when compared to Figure 4.8.

Simulation and Evaluation of Optimum Strategies

A system dynamics model of the government supply chain was developed to simulate the performance of the extended supply chain in the event of a sudden increase in demand, an occurrence that has been common in aviation parts over the past 5 years. Killingsworth, Chavez, and Martin provide a detailed description of the system dynamics model built to simulate the government ordering process.[24] An overview of the model is presented in Figure 4.11. The requirements-determination algorithms are included in the supply chain control center, through which buys and repairs are recommended. These recommendations are based on separate calculations embedded in individual feedback control loops in the model.

Figure 4.12 presents the structure in the system dynamics model for the procurement process. The total net assets are compared to the

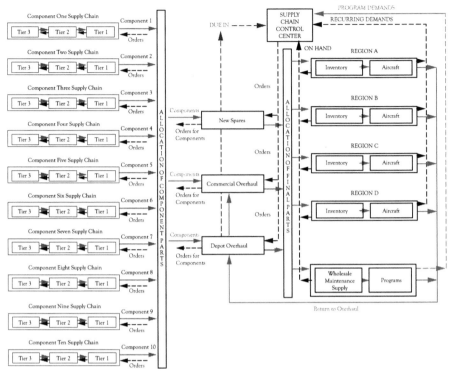

Figure 4.11. Overview of the multitier, multichannel system dynamics supply chain model.

procurement reorder point to determine whether a buy is recommended. If the total net assets are less than the procurement reorder point, the recommended buy is the difference between the two quantities plus the procurement cycle requirement, which is the amount of inventory needed to meet the forecasted demands until the next scheduled order. Once the manufacturing process is complete, the new products are added to the due-ins and calculated as part of the total net assets.

The recommended repair action is calculated similarly. The assets applicable for repair review are compared to the repair action point. If the assets are less than the repair action point, a maximum repair quantity is generated. In this case, however, the maximum repair quantity is compared to the available repairable carcasses to determine the recommended repair action. When the repairs are complete, the refurbished parts are

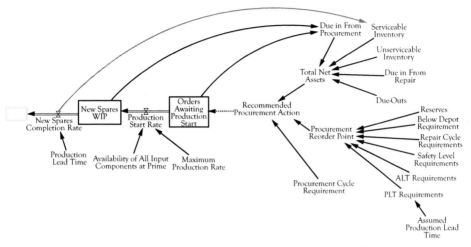

Figure 4.12. Recommended procurement action in system dynamics model.

added to the available inventory and calculated into the assets applicable for repair review.

Once the procurement and repair orders are placed through the OEM, the process for procuring the necessary components for each action is initiated, and orders are placed through independent suppliers. The flow for one of the components is depicted in Figure 4.13. Due to the risks involved, suppliers generally do not hold safety stock; thus, when an order is placed, substantial lead times affect the ability of each supplier to immediately respond. After the orders have flowed through each of the tiers and products have been shipped back through each of the subassemblies, the OEM completes the final assembly process. The final product is then shipped to the central inventory site before being distributed to one of the regional inventories. Each of the final parts is then pulled for use on an aircraft. Any damaged parts, less a percentage that are considered loss or scrap, are returned to the overhaul sites to begin the repair process.

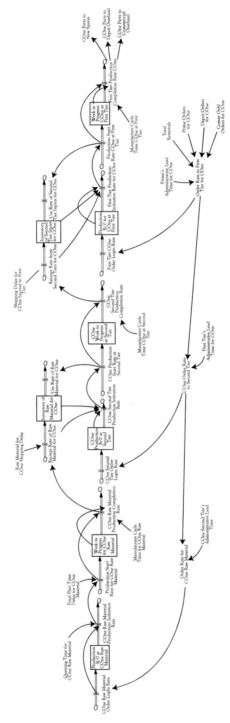

Figure 4.13. Supply chain tiers for component 1 system dynamics model.

Analysis and Simulation Results

A lack of safety stock combined with lengthy lead times causes the responsiveness of the government supply chain to suffer. Therefore, key objectives of the analysis were to (a) identify the current role of demand forecasting in supply planning, (b) develop a strategy for risk mitigation, (c) determine the recoverability of the government's requirements-determination process if safety stock were strategically placed throughout the supply chain, and (d) evaluate the impacts of implementing push-pull supply chain techniques in the government supply chain. The system dynamics model has been parameterized for the same helicopter blade used in the Inventory Analyst cases. The dynamic model was then used to test the performance of the optimal solutions under alternative cases.

Simulation Cases

The optimization results presented in Tables 4.1 to 4.4 were evaluated for the 2001–2013 timeframe using the system dynamics simulation model to explore the recovery rate of inventory levels when a sharp increase in demand occurs at the beginning of 2003. The cases are presented as follows:

> *Case 1.* OEM's PLT is 180 days and RLT is 90 days, the CST is
> 700 days, and no safety stock in the manufacturing tiers exists
> *Case 2.* OEM's PLT is 180 days and RLT is 90 days, the CST is
> 240 days, and safety stock is optimized
> *Case 3.* OEM's PLT is 180 days and RLT is 90 days, the CST is
> 30 days, and safety stock is optimized
> *Case 4.* OEM's PLT is 120 days and RLT is 60 days, the CST is
> 700 days, and no safety stock in the manufacturing tiers exists
> *Case 5.* OEM's PLT is 120 days and RLT is 60 days, the CST is
> 240 days, and safety stock is optimized
> *Case 6.* OEM's PLT is 120 days and RLT is 60 days, the CST is
> 30 days, and safety stock is optimized

Additional key assumptions for these cases include the following:

- Each component has a PLT between 6 and 16 months
- Overall PLT is 22 months and overall RLT is 11 months
- Demand begins at 14 units per month and increases to 20 units per month in 2003
- All overhaul is conducted commercially with a maximum overhaul capacity of 15 units per month
- New spare production is limited to 11 units per month
- Unserviceable recovery rate is 94%; that is, for every 100 parts issued, 94 are returned to the overhaul site
- Final recovery rate is 54%; that is, for every 100 parts returned, 54 can be repaired and reissued

The first case is the base scenario that represents the typical current conditions in which the OEM as well as the other suppliers throughout the supply chain carry no safety stock. Figure 4.14 shows the impact this limitation has on inventory levels when demand suddenly increases in 2003. Serviceable inventory is depleted for 5 years; thus, no issuable inventory is available on hand at the central inventory site during that time. Inventory at each of the regions is also exhausted for more than 2 years, and the supply system struggles to meet the new demand level. Stability does not

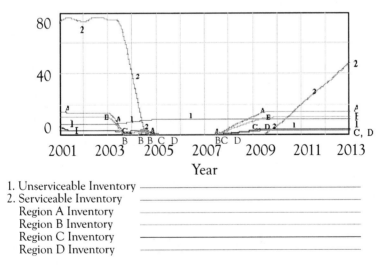

1. Unserviceable Inventory
2. Serviceable Inventory
   Region A Inventory
   Region B Inventory
   Region C Inventory
   Region D Inventory

Figure 4.14. Case 1 inventory levels with an increase in demand in 2003; no stocking in the manufacturing tiers exists.

return to the supply chain until well after the year 2013. The impact of this situation in the real world is profound when considered in context with wartime conditions such that lack of inventory affects the completion of missions, and ultimately human lives are at stake.[25]

Placing even limited inventory in a few strategic places, primarily at the tier 1 suppliers, produces significant improvements from the base case. Consider implementing placement of inventory levels corresponding to the quantities displayed in the optimization results in Figure 4.7. Not only does the CST drastically improve from approximately 2 years to under a year, but the response rate of the supply chain also improves dramatically. In this case, as depicted in Figure 4.15, serviceable inventory begins to recover in approximately 3.5 years rather than 5 years, and regional inventory recovers in approximately half the time as the base case (case 1). As discussed previously, this change can be accomplished with relatively little change in working capital. Thus even a minor investment can make a difference in the capabilities of the government supply chain.

Additional improvements can be made with a larger investment in working capital, as displayed in Table 4.2. Increasing this investment through strategic placement of additional safety stock at the

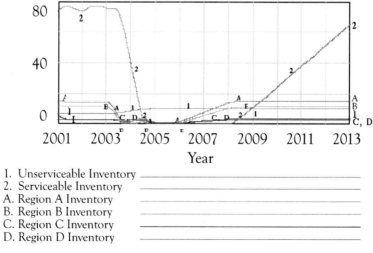

1. Unserviceable Inventory
2. Serviceable Inventory
A. Region A Inventory
B. Region B Inventory
C. Region C Inventory
D. Region D Inventory

Figure 4.15. Case 2 inventory levels with an increase in demand in 2003; stocking is optimized and the CST is 240 days.

OEM and the tier 1 suppliers further enhances the readiness of the supply chain. For example, placing inventory levels according to the Table 4.2, row 1 solution results in the reduction of the CST to 1 month, a substantial improvement from the current base case situation. Furthermore, the recoverability of the supply chain is improved. As shown in Figure 4.16, serviceable inventory recovers in half the amount of time as the base case, and regional inventory begins to recover almost immediately.

Despite the extent to which the responsiveness of the supply chain improves by implementing the inventory-optimization methodology, additional improvements are warranted due to the importance of meeting demand. Therefore, the next three cases assume the OEM can reduce its assembly time from 180 days to 120 days for new production and from 90 days to 60 days for overhaul. The first case assumes no safety stock in the manufacturing tiers. Figure 4.17 shows that this single change, although reducing the overall PLT by only 2 months, allows the recovery time of serviceable inventory to decrease by an entire year. In a similar fashion, regional inventories also recover a year earlier than the base case. In addition, as noted previously in Table 4.3, decreasing this

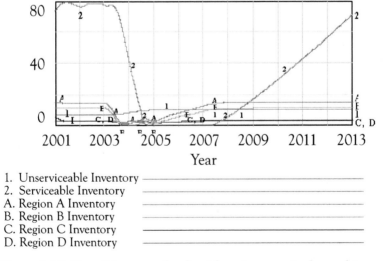

1. Unserviceable Inventory
2. Serviceable Inventory
A. Region A Inventory
B. Region B Inventory
C. Region C Inventory
D. Region D Inventory

Figure 4.16. Case 3 inventory levels with an increase in demand in 2003; stocking is optimized and the CST is 30 days.

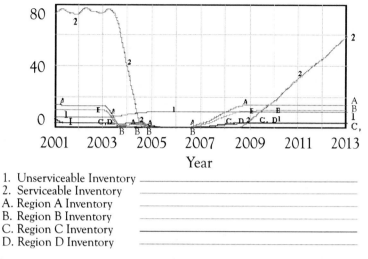

1. Unserviceable Inventory
2. Serviceable Inventory
A. Region A Inventory
B. Region B Inventory
C. Region C Inventory
D. Region D Inventory

Figure 4.17. Case 4 inventory levels with an increase in demand in 2003; no stocking in the manufacturing tiers exists.

assembly time reduces working capital substantially, and this savings can be reinvested in safety stock levels to further improve the readiness of the government supply chain.

Applying some of the working capital savings toward inventory optimization further helps the supply chain recover from sudden increases in demand. Figure 4.18 shows that the application of inventory-management policies across the supply chain produces important benefits to the customer. For example, maintaining safety stock levels as in Figure 4.19 allows the serviceable inventory to recover a year earlier than in the previous scenario. Regional inventory in this case begins to recover almost immediately. These are notable results compared to the base case, especially considering the working capital is still reduced from the original scenario.

Finally, applying additional working capital to inventory-optimization policies permits the CST to be reduced to 30 days, as noted in Table 4.4. Employing the Inventory Analyst solution shown in Table 4.4, row 1 to the stock levels across the supply chain substantially benefits the supply chain recovery rate by preventing a sudden increase in demand. The serviceable inventory levels begin recovery in a matter of months, and the regional inventory levels begin recovery immediately. The new demand

1. Unserviceable Inventory
2. Serviceable Inventory
A. Region A Inventory
B. Region B Inventory
C. Region C Inventory
D. Region D Inventory

Figure 4.18. Case 5 inventory levels with an increase in demand in 2003; stocking is optimized and the CST is 240 days.

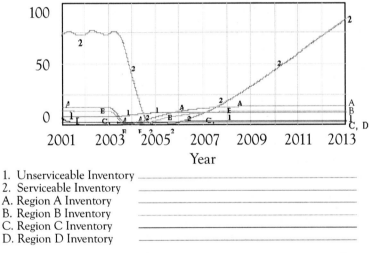

1. Unserviceable Inventory
2. Serviceable Inventory
A. Region A Inventory
B. Region B Inventory
C. Region C Inventory
D. Region D Inventory

Figure 4.19. Case 6 inventory levels with an increase in demand in 2003; stocking is optimized and the CST is 30 days.

level does not overwhelm the supply chain, and the entire system stabilizes by the year 2013. Working capital in this case is still reduced from the base case. This situation creates a supply chain that is much better suited to handle the volatility of demand and long lead times that are inherent in the aviation industry.

Conclusions

Supply chains for high-value aviation spare parts have experienced considerable problems in providing adequate and stable supply. Supply uncertainties such as long lead times and uncertain demand levels are a fundamental part of the problem. Holding larger and larger inventories of final goods is a very expensive method of counteracting this problem and is not fiscally viable. An improved alternative strategy can be developed by creating a push-pull boundary of optimized safety stock in the tiers of the manufacturing supply chain. This approach not only increases recovery rates from sudden shifts in demand but also reduces the amount of working capital invested to achieve desired service times. A simulation model of the extended supply chain has been used to demonstrate that push-pull boundaries enhance the ability of the supply chain to be adaptive and responsive and to efficiently mitigate the risks of forecast errors prevalent within the government requirements-determination process.

CHAPTER 5

Using System Dynamics to Estimate Reductions in Life-Cycle Costs Arising From Investments in Improved Reliability

Introduction

"Doing more with less" has become a long-running and recurring theme across the globe. Companies, government agencies, and even charities are being forced to deliver higher performance with reduced funding and capital.[1] This challenge is especially acute for the U.S. Department of Defense and the branches of the armed services where demands are great and budgets are tight. As long ago as 1995, Dr. Paul Kaminsky, then the Under Secretary of Defense for Acquisition and Technology, stated that a key goal "is a simple one of trying to do more with less."[2] This objective has steadily become more critical over the last 15 years and has led to ongoing efforts to achieve efficiencies while at the same time maintaining availability and system readiness. Because typically the costs to operate, maintain, and dispose of a weapon system account for about 72% of the total cost of ownership, much effort has focused on these expenditures.[3] The Department of Defense (DoD) Reliability, Availability, Maintainability, and Cost Rationale Report Manual states the issues succinctly:

> The Department of Defense (DoD) needs to acquire reliable and maintainable products that are of high quality and readily

available to satisfy user requirements in meeting mission capability and operational tasks. The Department must acquire these products at the most reasonable cost to the taxpayer. The cost to the government, however, is not just computed by the procurement costs, but also must balance the long-term costs incurred in maintenance, driven by reliability, availability, and other factors throughout the system life cycle.[4]

Improvements in reliability have multiple cost-saving impacts such as fewer parts to buy and overhaul, smaller inventories of replacement parts, fewer inspections, reduced maintenance hours and down time, reduced transportation costs to ship replacement parts, and so on. Nevertheless, recent research found the following to be the case:

Test results since 2001 show that roughly fifty percent of DoD's programs are unsuitable at the time of initial operational test and evaluation, because they do not achieve reliability goals. This represents a significant and alarming change in the number of programs found unsuitable as compared to historical levels. Because reliability is a prime determinant of long-term support costs, delivered reliability so far off the mark has serious consequences for both operational suitability and affordability.[5]

Because of the strong tie between reliability and sustainment costs, DoD Director of Operational Test and Evaluation Charles E. McQueary sponsored research to investigate the empirical relationships between reliability investments, improvements in reliability, and life-cycle support costs. In this research, a preliminary relationship between investment in reliability (normalized by average production unit cost) and achieved reliability improvement was developed. This relationship is presented in Figure 5.1 and is taken from a presentation delivered by McQueary.

As an illustrative data point on the graph of Figure 5.1, the research determined that the Predator program invested a total cumulative amount of $39.1 million in reliability investments over a 9-year period. The ratio of this investment to the average production unit cost (APUC) of $4.2 million is 9.3 and is the value of the x-axis for the Predator data point. The research also determined that the overall failure rate of the

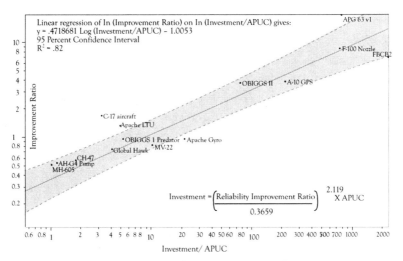

Figure 5.1. Empirical relationship between reliability improvements and reliability investments.

Source: Life Cycle Cost Savings by Improving Reliability, by Dr. Charles E. McQueary Director, Operational Test and Evaluation, 2009, http://www.gw-itea.org/documents/McQuearyGW-ITEA luncheonPresentationJan2009.ppt

Predator was reduced by 48.1%, resulting in an overall improvement in mean time between failures (MTBF) from 40 hours in fiscal year (FY)98 to 77 hours in FY06, or a 92.5% improvement in reliability. This is the *y*-axis point for the Predator. The other data points on this graph reflect the results of similar analysis.

It should be noted that this chart relates reliability investments to reliability improvements but does not take the next step and relate investments in reliability to reductions in life-cycle costs. Additional research is focusing on that next step using the Cost Analysis Strategy Assessment (CASA) model, a total life-cycle cost-analysis tool, and other analytical techniques.[6] Such models give estimates for changes in 20-year support costs based on a variety of input assumptions, including changes in reliability. These models, however, do not give indications of changes in readiness levels or of payback time for the investment. According to the Department of the Army Economic Analysis Manual, the breakeven point (payback period) is an important metric for investments. For example, two investments might have similar benefit-cost ratios or similar savings-to-investment ratios, but if one has a substantially faster payback, then it is the superior investment. Both the readiness and time-dynamic aspects of reliability investments need to be included in a benefits analysis.

One approach to investigating sustainment costs that incorporates both readiness and time of payback is to view the support process as an ongoing enterprise supply chain that provides new parts, repair, support, maintenance, and the like over the operating life cycle. Improvements in reliability clearly affect the operational aspects of the supply chain through reductions in removals, overhaul requirements, new spare acquisitions, shipment of replacements, and all the associated and related costs. Simulation of this enterprise using a dynamic-modeling approach can establish a relationship between improvements in reliability and reduced operating costs as well as indicating changes in readiness levels and time of payback.

Model Description

An overview of the supply chain for high-value aviation parts is shown in Figure 5.2. This diagram illustrates the flow of parts from new production and overhaul to the final customer. The overall supply chain process is managed in a feedback form by the government's ordering or requirements-determination process. These algorithms are typically embedded in a computerized process utilized by item managers, such as the Army's Supply Control Study. Based on the calculated recommendations, repair action or procurement action will be initiated. This process, or something similar, is used by most government and defense supply chains for high-value parts.[7]

By systematically comparing current levels of inventory, due-ins, due-outs, and historical demand levels, the ordering process determines the recommended buys and repairs. The demand for a part is driven by the total number of installed parts, monthly operating hours, and failure rate per part per operating hour, sometimes expressed as a mean time between failures. The supply of parts comes from three possible sources: production of new items, commercial overhaul of damaged parts, and government overhaul of damaged parts. Once the production or overhaul process is completed, parts are transferred to the central distribution inventory. Each region has an inventory of key spare parts, and these inventories are replenished from the central distribution inventory. Parts

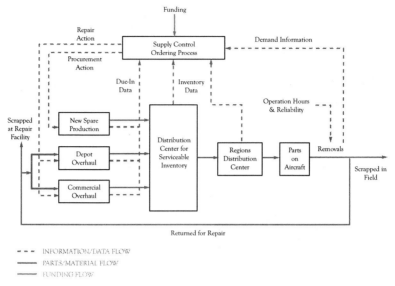

Figure 5.2. Overview of supply chain model.

excessively damaged and unable to be repaired may be scrapped at two different points once they are removed from the aircraft. The first possibility is for parts to be scrapped in the field and not returned for overhaul. The second possibility is for parts to be scrapped at the repair facility, either a depot or a commercial manufacturer.

Several levels of calculation are incorporated into the supply-control ordering process to determine recommended buys and repairs.[8] The determination process calculates the procurement action for new spare parts by calculating the difference between the procurement reorder point and the total net assets, and then adding the procurement cycle requirement and the inventory necessary to meet demands until the next scheduled order. Total net assets are calculated from due-ins from procurement and repair plus inventories, less due-outs. The procurement reorder point is based on targeted reserves and safety levels. Within the model, orders that are placed with the original equipment manufacturer (OEM) enter production subject to a maximum production rate and availability of all the required components. Production is completed after a manufacturing lead time. After production, these new parts flow into the distribution center for serviceable inventory. Figure 5.3 illustrates the recommended new spares procurement action.

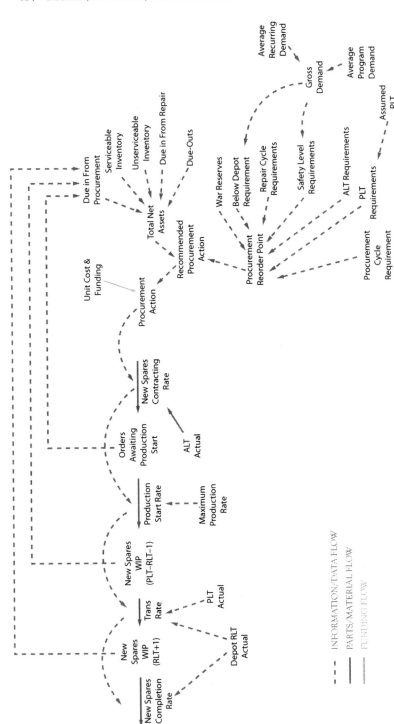

Figure 5.3. Recommended new spares procurement action.

The determination for recommended repair action differs in an important way from the determination of the recommended procurement action. First, the maximum recommended repair action is calculated by subtracting the assets available for repair, including overhaul and procurement work in process less due-outs, from the repair action point, calculated with reserve levels and safety requirements. This process is largely driven by historical demands. In the second step, the maximum recommended repair action, however, is then limited by the unserviceable inventory on hand. A damaged part must be available for repair or overhaul to take place. The potentially constrained repair order is allocated between government depot and commercial overhaul according to capacity levels at each location. The overhaul rates may also be limited by production capacity levels. Similar to procurement production, once overhaul is complete, the part is transported to the distribution center for serviceable inventory. Figure 5.4 illustrates the process for calculating the recommended repair action.

Upon arrival at the distribution center for serviceable inventory, all parts, both new and repaired, are available for shipment to the regional inventory centers.

The regional inventory center orders parts from the central distribution center to replenish that inventory being used to replace removed parts. The monthly removals are dependent on the number of parts in service (i.e., number installed on aircraft), the monthly operational hours

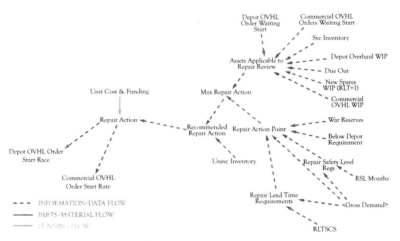

Figure 5.4. Recommended repair action.

(i.e., monthly flight hours), and failure rate per monthly operational hour. Hence if reliability is improved, the failure rate per flight hour is reduced, demand is reduced, and pull from inventories is reduced. This leads to reduced orders for new spares and overhaul. This high-level view of the model structure is shown in Figure 5.5.

The objectives of this research are to determine how investments in reliability improvement can reduce life-cycle costs and improve readiness. It is assumed in the model that the investment occurs over a 3-year period that includes design, manufacturing, test, and certification. Shorter or longer investment scenarios are easily included and examined in the model structure. Figure 5.6 illustrates this structure for the simulation and the factors involved in calculating annual current-dollar, constant-dollar, and discounted-dollar expenditures as well as life-cycle cumulative costs. The figure also illustrates how the discount and inflation rates are used in the calculation for constant dollars (constant-year dollars are the

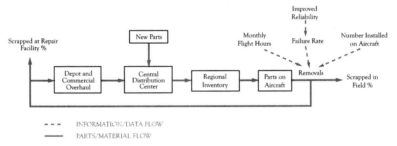

Figure 5.5. Reliability, flight hours, and removals.

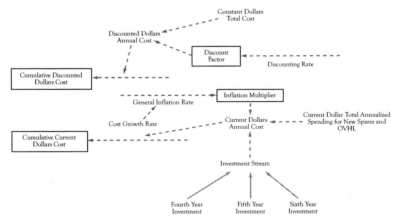

Figure 5.6. Investment for improved reliability.

result of having the effects of inflation removed; constant-year dollars are always associated with a base year), discounted dollars (discounted dollars are the present value of a cost made in the future), and current dollars (current-year dollars are expressed in the value of the year in which a cost is expected to occur and therefore reflect the effects of inflation).

The investment in reliability impacts the spending amounts for each year after the new, improved part is introduced, depending on the degree of reliability improvement for the part and any changes in the unit cost of the part. It may very well be the case that the improved part will have a higher production cost, and the model enables the investigation of trade-off between improved reliability, higher unit cost, and reduced demand. Figure 5.7 illustrates the calculation in the model of cumulative spending and annualized spending.

Evaluation of Alternative Investments

The key objectives of the analysis were twofold:

1. To determine the reductions in life-cycle costs and payback periods for investments in reliability using "what if" assumptions relating the improved reliability and the assumed level of investment. In these analyses, payback is determined and life-cycle costs are calculated assuming, for example, that a $10 million investment will generate a 10% improvement in reliability. The simulation can

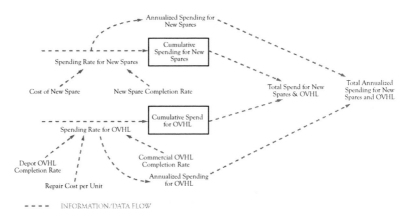

Figure 5.7. Cumulative and annualized spending.

then be conducted assuming that the $10 million produces a 20% increase in reliability. These types of analyses allow one to determine the required reliability improvement of an investment such that an adequate return is generated through reductions in life-cycle costs. This enables a business case analysis to be completed for a proposed program.

2. To determine the reductions in life-cycle costs and payback periods for investments in reliability using empirical data developed in previous DoD research that relates investment as a percentage of unit cost to improvements in reliability. This analysis can then supplement and support a business case analysis as conducted earlier.

In the first part of the investigation, the model structure was parameterized for a major repairable helicopter part. The simulation begins 1 January 2001. Demands in 2001 and 2002 were fairly stable, as were inventories. However, with the onset of the conflict in Iraq, demands rose sharply in 2003 and have remained elevated. As a result of the increased demands, inventories of many aviation parts were seriously depleted for a period of 3 to 4 years. For the part in question, the production lead time was roughly 24 months. Because of this long lead time, inventories for this part were reduced to near zero levels. A key validation test of the model was the ability to capture these dynamics. In the simulations for exploring improvements in reliability, it is assumed that investments in reliability were initiated in 2003 and extended through the end of 2005, a 3-year investment period. The improved part becomes available at the beginning of 2006. The time span for this simulation was selected in order to simulate an initial steady level in demand, then a significant surge in demand, and to investigate the likely impacts of improved reliability on inventory recovery and cost reductions.

All cases assume stable demand levels from 2001 to the beginning of 2003. In addition, all cases include a rise in demand beginning in 2003 due to an increase in operating flight hours. In 2003, flight hours increase from 14 hours per aircraft per month to 18 hours per aircraft per month. Figure 5.8 presents operating hours per month over the simulation. It is important to note that this assumption for flight hours is the major external assumption driving the simulation and that this assumption can be easily altered.

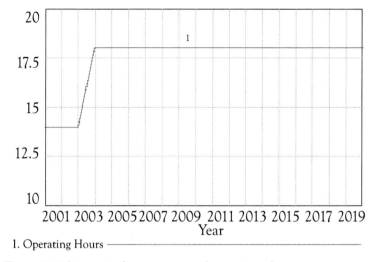

1. Operating Hours ————————————————————————————

Figure 5.8 Operating hours per month per aircraft.

The flight-hour assumption and the failure rate per flight hour yields an initial monthly demand of 11, which increases to 14 following the increase in flight hours. In addition to these recurring demands, it is assumed in the model that the part has an initial monthly program demand of 3 and that the program demand increases to 5 during 2003. These program demands arise through programs such as reset

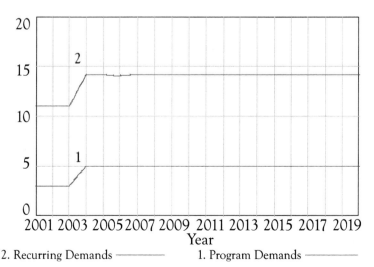

2. Recurring Demands ——————   1. Program Demands ——————

Figure 5.9 Monthly recurring demands and program demands.

and recapitalization and are independent of flight hours. The demand assumptions are shown in Figure 5.9. For the simulation, it is assumed that with growing demands, an investment program is undertaken to improve reliability.

Note again that for those cases assuming a reliability investment, the investment is equally divided over 3 years (2003–2005 in these simulations). Starting in 2006, the introduction of the part with improved reliability begins to reduce demands, support inventory levels, and reduce procurement and repair actions. It is assumed in the model that the new parts are introduced through attrition. That is, as older parts are removed, they are replaced with the improved part. It is assumed that the removed parts that are not scrapped are transformed in the overhaul process to the part configuration with higher reliability. Current research is addressing the case in which this improvement is not possible in the overhaul process. The complete turnover in parts requires approximately 8 years, given the demand level in Figure 5.9. Thus the overall transition to the improved MTBF occurs over that period of time.

In some of the alternative cases with improved reliability, an increase in the cost of the part is assumed. In these cases, the cost increase takes effect in 2006 as the new parts are introduced. Table 5.1 presents the key assumptions for five reliability cases to be analyzed through simulation.

Evaluation of Investment in Reliability

Case 1. Base case analysis: no investment in reliability, no improvement in reliability, and no increase in parts cost; this simulation should reflect actual supply chain performance

Table 5.1. Cases for Improved Reliability

Case	Reliability investment	Improvement in reliability (MTBF; %)	Parts cost increase (%)
1	No	0	0
2	Yes	33	0
3	Yes	33	15
4	Yes	50	0
5	Yes	50	15

Case 1 was conducted to provide a base case for inventory levels and procurement and repair actions over time. Cases 2 to 5 with improved reliability may then be compared to this base case. Figures 5.10 to 5.12 present the results of case 1. As seen in Figure 5.10, the surge in demand in 2003 causes a dramatic reduction in serviceable inventories. This decline in inventories creates back orders in the system, as orders cannot be completed due to lack of supply in inventory. In Figure 5.11, new procurement remains steady for the first 4 years but ultimately ramps up due to the increase in demand arising from the greater number of flight hours. The delay in this ramp-up arises from the fact that the requirements-determination process uses a 24-month rolling average for demand calculations. This rolling average only slowly reflects the higher demand levels. In Figure 5.11, the small tick marks or spikes labeled 3 represent procurement orders that arise as the total net assets level drops below the requirements objective. In Figure 5.12, the max repair activity rises sharply due to increased demand. The maximum repair activity represents the repair action that the system would optimally like to realize, but that action cannot be executed due to the lack of unserviceable inventory. Even though the max repair action is quite high, only the available unserviceable parts can be repaired, and the repair action remains at a modest level constrained by the flow of returning parts for overhaul.

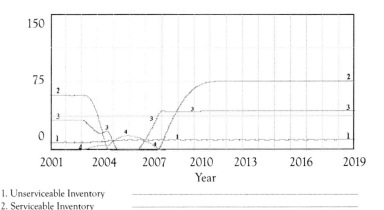

1. Unserviceable Inventory
2. Serviceable Inventory
3. Available Inventory at Regions
4. Backorders

Figure 5.10. Case 1 inventory levels.

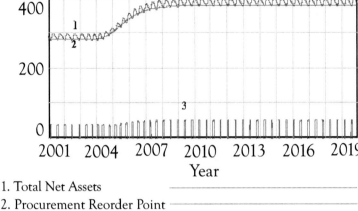

1. Total Net Assets

2. Procurement Reorder Point

3. Procurement Action

Figure 5.11. Case 1 procurement action.

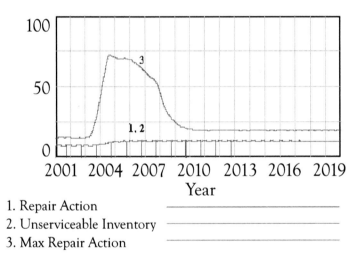

1. Repair Action

2. Unserviceable Inventory

3. Max Repair Action

Figure 5.12. Case 1 repair action.

Notice that although demands increased sharply in 2003, procurement and repair actions ramp up slowly. This is again because the typical DoD requirements-determination process uses a 24-month rolling average as the basis for demand forecasting. This lagged average introduces a substantial delay in the process and, when combined with a 24-month production lead time, creates a situation where inventories are rapidly pulled down following a sustained surge in demand, and inventory recovery is very slow.

Case 2. Investment made to improve reliability, 33% improvement in reliability, and no increase in unit part cost

Case 3. Investment made to improve reliability, 33% improvement in reliability, and a 15% increase in unit part cost

Cases 2 and 3 examine the impacts of investments in reliability on demands, inventories, readiness, and life-cycle costs relative to the base case. Figures 5.13 to 5.15 present the results of these cases. It should be noted that although case 3 involves a percentage increase in unit part cost after the investment period, inventory levels, procurement actions, and repair actions are the same in both cases because it is assumed that funding is available to make the recommended buys and overhauls. The increase in cost of the part does, however, impact total life-cycle cost and reduces the return in case 3. Figure 5.13 presents simulation results for inventories for cases 2 and 3. As may be seen, with the more reliable part entering service in 2006, inventories recover faster because of improved reliability and reduced demands. In fact, because of the long production lead time and demand averaging, orders continue to be made at a higher than necessary level and inventories overshoot the objective before falling back to the steady goal appropriate for the new reduced demand levels. The unserviceable inventory level also rises because fewer parts require repair action due to improved reliability and reduced demand. Figure 5.14 shows a reduction in orders for new spares (the tick marks labeled as

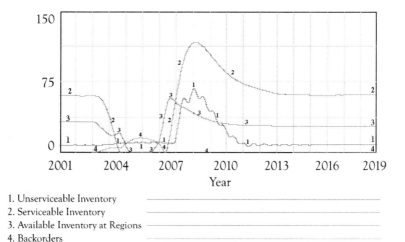

1. Unserviceable Inventory
2. Serviceable Inventory
3. Available Inventory at Regions
4. Backorders

Figure 5.13. Cases 2 and 3 inventory levels.

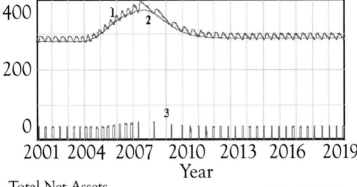

1. Total Net Assets
2. Procurement Reorder Point
3. Procurement Action

Figure 5.14. Cases 2 and 3 procurement action.

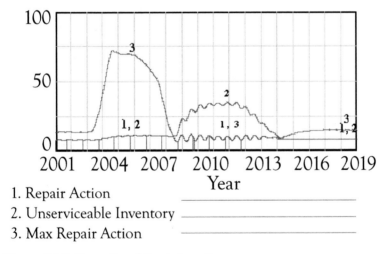

1. Repair Action
2. Unserviceable Inventory
3. Max Repair Action

Figure 5.15. Cases 2 and 3 repair action.

3 are buys). Following the introduction of the improved part, the interval between orders increases because the parts are now more reliable and monthly removals are reduced. Lastly, Figure 5.15 shows a ramp-up in unserviceable inventory after the investment period for cases 2 and 3. As stated, the improvement in reliability causes the unserviceable inventory level to rise due to reduced repair actions because of longer-lasting parts. Thus unserviceable inventory will build as fewer parts are overhauled. This may be seen in the lower levels of repair activity.

Case 4. Investment made to improve reliability, 50% improvement in reliability, and no increase in unit part cost

Case 5. Investment made to improve reliability, 50% improvement in reliability, and a 15% increase in unit part cost

Cases 4 and 5 were conducted to assess the impacts of even greater improvements in reliability. Figures 5.16 to 5.18 present the results for cases 4 and 5. Figure 5.16 shows that a 50% improvement in reliability greatly increases the sharpness and rapidity of inventory recovery. Also, the total number of back orders is lower than in any other cases. Figure 5.17

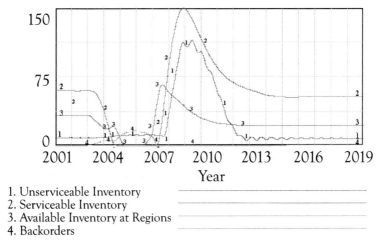

1. Unserviceable Inventory
2. Serviceable Inventory
3. Available Inventory at Regions
4. Backorders

Figure 5.16. Cases 4 and 5 inventory levels.

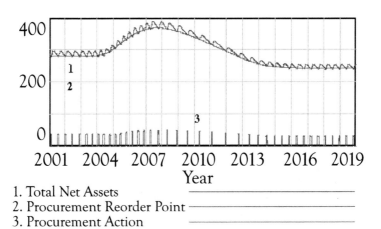

1. Total Net Assets
2. Procurement Reorder Point
3. Procurement Action

Figure 5.17. Cases 4 and 5 procurement action.

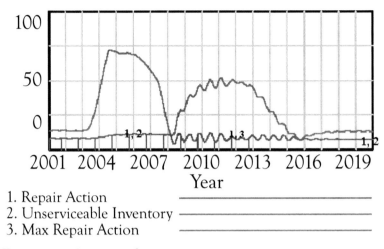

1. Repair Action
2. Unserviceable Inventory
3. Max Repair Action

Figure 5.18. Cases 4 and 5 repair action.

shows that in this simulation, once the investment period ends, the new improved parts are shipped in 2006 and 2007 at close to historical levels. Since parts are lasting longer, however, fewer new parts are required to meet the requirements objective (RO). As a result, procurement actions are less frequent from 2008 to 2013. They then settle to a lower level that reflects the lower monthly demands. In a similar fashion, Figure 5.18 shows that after the investment period, repair actions slow for 1 year, again because of reduced demand arising from increased reliability in parts, and then repair actions become somewhat less stable as the system adjusts to the new demand levels. Also, unserviceable inventory rises higher than in any of the previous cases because less repair activity is required.

Figure 5.19 presents the current dollars (i.e., inflated dollars) annual spend on parts over the course of the simulation for all five cases. After the investment period, all cases show significant savings in annual spending relative to case 1. Case 5 shows an annual savings of $60 million for this single part in 2020. Figure 5.20 presents the current dollars cumulative spend over the 10-year period of the simulation. For case 5, the cumulative savings are roughly $600 million over this life-cycle assessment. It is clear that the greater the reliability improvement, the greater the total cost savings, and these savings are significant.

Figure 5.21 presents current dollars annual spending amounts for all five cases. For cases 2 through 5, the savings columns present the

Current Dollars Annual Spend

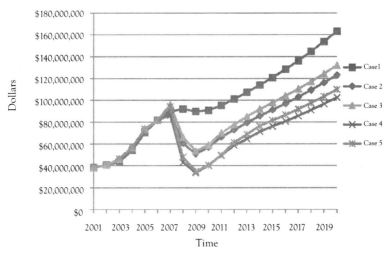

Figure 5.19. Current dollars annual spend cases for improved reliability.

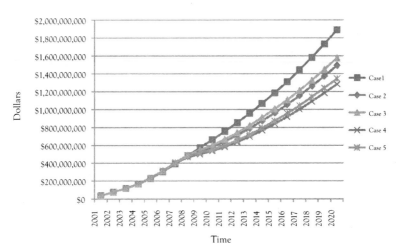

Figure 5.20. Current dollars cumulative spend cases for improved reliability.

reduction in spending from case 1 over the 20-year period. The shading denotes the years in which an investment is made for improved reliability. The table also provides the payback or breakeven (B/E) point in number of years. The lower portion of the chart presents the payback ratio for the investment. This final financial metric is obtained by dividing the

Year	Case 1	Case 2		Case 3		Case 4		Case 5	
	(0%, 0%)	(33%, 0%)	Savings	(33%, 15%)	Savings	(50%, 0%)	Savings	(50%, 15%)	Savings
2001	$38.14	$38.14	$0.00	$38.14	$0.00	$38.14	$0.00	$38.14	$0.00
2002	$40.64	$40.64	$0.00	$40.64	$0.00	$40.64	$0.00	$40.64	$0.00
2003	$43.37	$43.37	$0.00	$43.37	$0.00	$43.37	$0.00	$43.37	$0.00
2004	$53.93	$53.93	$0.00	$53.93	$0.00	$53.93	$0.00	$53.93	$0.00
2005	$70.47	$70.47	$0.00	$70.47	$0.00	$70.47	$0.00	$70.47	$0.00
2006	$81.79	$81.79	$0.00	$81.79	$0.00	$81.79	$0.00	$81.79	$0.00
2007	$89.49	$88.60	$0.89	$96.28	-$6.79	$88.15	$1.34	$95.79	-$6.30
2008	$92.00	$84.23	$7.77	$91.23	$0.77	$77.36	$14.64	$83.95	$8.05
2009	$89.61	$71.92	$17.69	$77.37	$12.24	$62.84	$26.77	$67.47	$22.14
2010	$90.79	$68.14	$22.65	$72.64	$18.15	$57.35	$33.44	$60.65	$30.14
2011	$95.14	$67.49	$27.65	$71.60	$23.54	$53.33	$41.81	$55.92	$39.22
2012	$100.10	$68.23	$31.87	$72.18	$27.92	$51.13	$48.97	$53.27	$46.83
2013	$107.26	$72.91	$34.35	$77.01	$30.25	$55.26	$52.00	$57.39	$49.87
2014	$113.85	$80.41	$33.44	$85.18	$28.67	$63.11	$50.74	$66.02	$47.83
2015	$120.88	$87.46	$33.42	$93.20	$27.68	$71.85	$49.03	$75.95	$44.93
2016	$128.33	$94.38	$33.95	$101.01	$27.32	$77.45	$50.88	$82.61	$45.72
2017	$136.29	$101.83	$34.46	$109.16	$27.13	$84.23	$52.06	$90.15	$46.14
2018	$144.73	$108.92	$35.81	$116.83	$27.90	$90.47	$54.26	$96.93	$47.80
2019	$153.65	$115.94	$37.71	$124.37	$29.28	$96.44	$57.21	$103.36	$50.29
2020	$163.15	$123.11	$40.04	$132.07	$31.08	$102.48	$60.67	$109.83	$53.32
Cumulative savings		$391.70		$305.14		$593.82		$525.98	
Investment (over 3-year period: years 2004–2006									
$3 million	B/E (years)		2.27		3.74		2.11		3.06
$6 million	B/E (years)		2.66		3.98		2.32		3.19
$9 million	B/E (years)		3.02		4.15		2.52		3.33
$12 million	B/E (years)		3.19		4.32		2.73		3.46

Figure 5.21. Annual spending and savings for cases with improved reliability.

Year	Case 1	Case 2		Case 3		Case 4		Case 5	
	(0%, 0%)	(33%, 0%)	Savings	(33%, 15%)	Savings	(50%, 0%)	Savings	(50%, 15%)	Savings
Benefit/investment ratio									
$3 million		129.57		100.71		196.94		174.33	
$6 million		64.28		49.86		97.97		86.66	
$9 million		42.52		32.90		64.98		57.44	
$12 million		31.64		24.43		48.49		42.83	

Current dollar annual spending and savings

Base scrap/loss rate 35%, 15%

(% Improvement in reliability, % parts cost increase)

Note: All costs in millions

Figure 5.21. Annual spending and savings for cases with improved reliability (continued).

current dollars cumulative savings by the total investment. The payback ratio demonstrates the time significance of the cost reduction for process improvement. For example, the results from case 2 illustrate current dollars cumulative savings of roughly $75 million in the 6 years (2006 through the end of 2011) following the investment period. The chart indicates that a $3 million investment spread equally over 2003, 2004, and 2005 would be recaptured in 2.27 years after the investment period ends. A $6 million investment spread equally over those same years would allow for a payback period of 2.66 years. To evaluate the alternative cases with different investment amounts and payback periods, investment amounts of $3 million, $6 million, $9 million, and $12 million were used. Cases 3, 4, and 5 also exhibit quick payback or breakeven time in years. These results indicate the strong potential for reduced operations and support (O&S) costs through reliability investments.

Evaluation of Reliability Investment from Empirical Data

In the second part of the investigation, the model structure was again parameterized for a major repairable helicopter part, but rather than for a variable demand rate, a 20-year steady-state life cycle was assumed. Moreover, this part of the analysis utilizes an empirical relationship between reliability investment and reliability improvement.

As discussed in the introduction to this chapter, Logistics Management Institute (LMI) with the sponsorship of DoD developed a linear regression equation relating investments to reliability improvements. This linear regression is presented in Figure 5.1. The regression relates the investment divided by the APUC to the reliability improvement ratio, which is the percentage increase in reliability. The likely improvement in reliability arising from a certain investment can be determined using this linear regression. It should be noted that in Figure 5.1 the cases in the lower range of the investment ratio tend to be for large systems or aircraft. As a result, ratios of 1 to 10 may not be appropriate for major repairable parts. Rather, ratios ranging from 20 to 1000 may be more appropriate for investments to improve the reliability of major assemblies and parts. This upper range of investment ratios is used in this study.

Table 5.2 presents four cases developed using the empirical regression between investment and reliability improvement. For this part of the analysis, case 6 represents the base case before any investment in reliability improvement is made. It represents "business as usual." The investment/APUC column gives for each case the ratio for investment to APUC. For example, in case 7 with an APUC of $250,000, an investment of $5 million yields an investment ratio of 20. For case 8, an investment of $7.5 million yields a ratio of 30, and for case 9 an investment of $10 million yields a ratio of 40. In the simulation analyses, the total investment amount is divided equally over 3 years (years 1 through 3 of the simulation). The

Table 5.2. Cases for Improved Reliability Using Empirical Data

Case	Investment/ APUC	Increase in MTBF (%)	Reduction in failure rate per flight hour (%)
6	0	0	0.0
7	20	150	60.0
8	30	200	66.7
9	40	225	69.2

percentage increase in the MTBF column is calculated from the linear regression example provided in Figure 5.1. The final column provides the reduction in failure rate per flight hour from the base failure rate. The failures per flight hour is inversely related to the MTBF.

Figures 5.22 to 5.24 present the inventory levels, procurement actions, and repair actions over the course of the 20-year simulation for case 6, the 20-year base case. With constant demands, all inventory levels and procurement and repair actions remain constant over the simulation as would be expected.

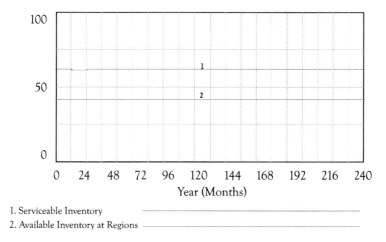

1. Serviceable Inventory
2. Available Inventory at Regions

Figure 5.22. Case 6 inventory levels.

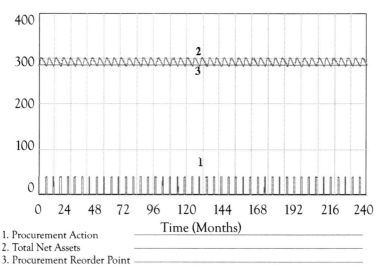

1. Procurement Action
2. Total Net Assets
3. Procurement Reorder Point

Figure 5.23. Case 6 procurement action.

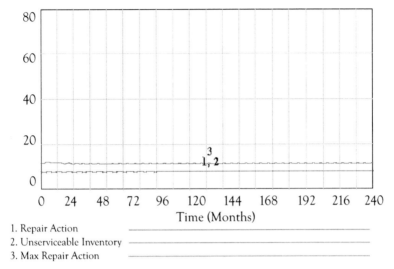

1. Repair Action
2. Unserviceable Inventory
3. Max Repair Action

Figure 5.24. Case 6 repair action.

Figures 5.25 to 5.27 present the results for case 7 with reliability improvement of 150%. This results in monthly removals dropping by more than half—in fact, a reduction of 60% over the introduction period of roughly 8 years. As seen in Figure 5.25, inventory levels climb after the investment period (years 1 to 3), and the new part begins introduction. The growth in inventory is a result of parts arriving out of

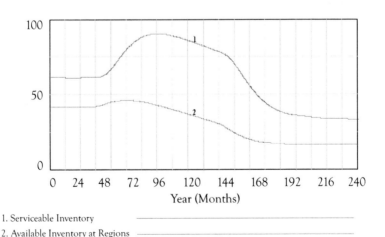

1. Serviceable Inventory
2. Available Inventory at Regions

Figure 5.25. Case 7 inventory levels.

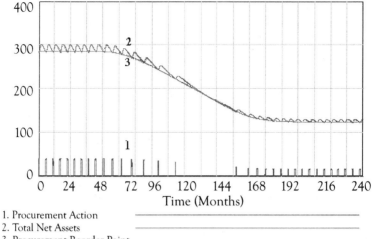

1. Procurement Action
2. Total Net Assets
3. Procurement Reorder Point

Figure 5.26. Case 7 procurement action.

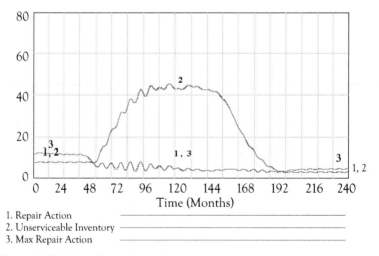

1. Repair Action
2. Unserviceable Inventory
3. Max Repair Action

Figure 5.27. Case 7 repair action.

a 2-year production pipeline into an environment of reduced demand. The model incorporates and simulates the actions of the requirements-determination process, which uses a 24-month rolling average for demand. As a result, recommended procurement and repair actions do not begin to slow down in the simulation until there has been more than a year of reduced demands. Figure 5.26 presents procurement actions. It is important to note that 6 years after the introduction of the new improved part, new procurement halts for 3 years so as to work off the accumulated inventory. Even as new procurement action begins to pick up, fewer numbers of new parts are ordered than initial levels. Figure 5.27 shows the slow reduction in repair action and the buildup of the unserviceable inventory. This growth arises because fewer parts are inducted into the overhaul process due to longer-lasting parts and reduced demands.

Figures 5.28 to 5.30 present the results for case 8, assuming a 200% improvement in reliability. Figure 5.28 illustrates the inventory levels, which, similar to case 7, become significantly higher following the investment period. Again, this is the result of reduced demands and historical orders emerging from the production pipeline. As parts become more reliable and last longer, serviceable inventories, unserviceable inventories, and available inventories at the regional facilities increase substantially. Figure 5.29 presents the procurement action over time. The orders for new parts halt for 5 years as the demand is consistently met through inventories and overhaul. As shown in Figure 5.30, repair orders are reduced over time, and it requires a number of years to reduce the buildup of unserviceable inventory.

Figures 5.31 to 5.33 present the results for case 9 with a 225% improvement in reliability. Results are similar except that the buildup

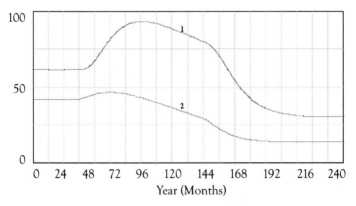

1. Serviceable Inventory

2. Available Inventory at Regions

Figure 5.28. Case 8 inventory levels.

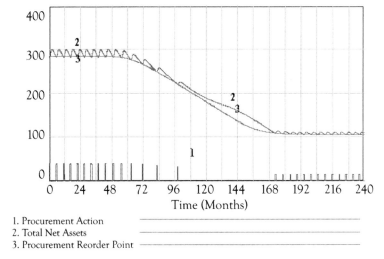

1. Procurement Action
2. Total Net Assets
3. Procurement Reorder Point

Figure 5.29. Case 8 procurement action.

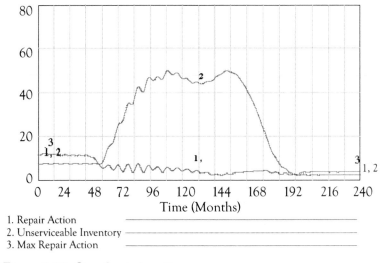

1. Repair Action
2. Unserviceable Inventory
3. Max Repair Action

Figure 5.30. Case 8 repair action.

of inventories is greater and procurement is halted for a more extended period of time.

Figure 5.34 presents the annual spend in current dollars for the four cases. The investment expenditures during years 1 through 3 are included in the spend for cases 7, 8, and 9. Note that the spend for the improved reliability cases drops significantly in the years following the introduction

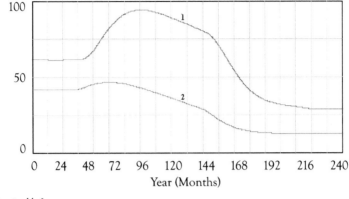

1. Serviceable Inventory

2. Available Inventory at Regions

Figure 5.31. Case 9 inventory levels.

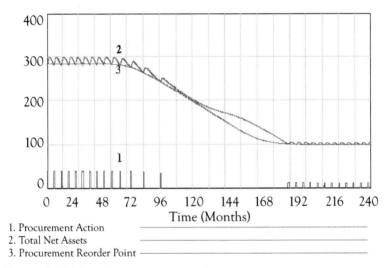

1. Procurement Action

2. Total Net Assets

3. Procurement Reorder Point

Figure 5.32. Case 9 procurement action.

of the new part. This drop is associated with the sharp reductions in new procurement that occur several years following introduction. When procurement begins to be required again, the spend begins a slow climb. In all cases, however, the annual spend is roughly $60 million lower than the base cost in case 6.

Figure 5.35 presents cumulative spend in current dollars for the four cases. The reduction in spending from the base over the 20-year life cycle

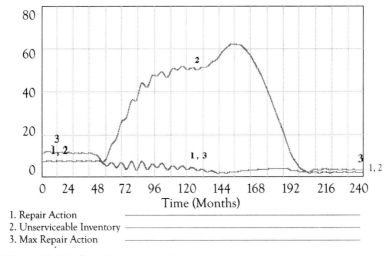

1. Repair Action
2. Unserviceable Inventory
3. Max Repair Action

Figure 5.33. Case 9 repair action.

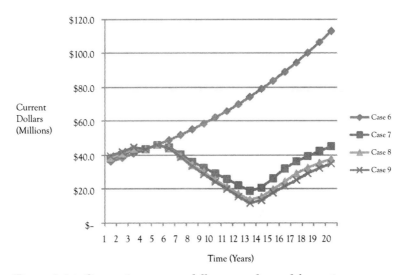

Figure 5.34. Comparing current dollar annual spend for various cases.

ranges from $700 million to $800 million, thus demonstrating the substantial returns provided by the investments that ranged from $5 million to $10 million for a part costing $250,000.

Table 5.3 and Figure 5.36 present a cumulative life-cycle summary for cases 6, 7, 8, and 9. As may be seen, paybacks from investment in reliability can be very substantial and very attractive. Note that the investment

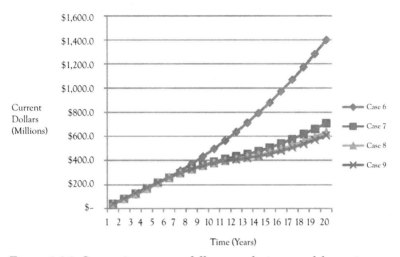

Figure 5.35. Comparing current dollar cumulative spend for various cases.

amount is included in the costs of the alternatives. As Figure 5.36 illustrates, there is a point where the percentage in cost reduction begins to level off and decline. Savings reach an upper limit of approximately 50% of base costs and then decline as the investment amount increases and ultimately increases the total costs. Nevertheless, for the part with APUC of $250,000, investments in improved reliability on the order of $7.5 to $10 million generate estimated life-cycle cost reductions of roughly $600 million in current dollars; this may be interpreted approximately as needing to buy 1300 fewer parts over the 20-year life cycle.

As may be seen in Figure 5.36, there appears to be an investment "sweet spot" that exists in a range of (Inv/APUC) ratio between 50 and 100.

Figure 5.37 presents the benefits (i.e., savings) to investment ratio as a function of the investment ratio in constant dollars. This reinforces the finding that an investment ratio exceeding 100 produces sharply lower returns.

Impacts on Readiness and Availability

Although the discussion so far has focused on economics—namely investments, costs, and savings—improvements in reliability can also have significant impacts on aircraft availability and readiness. Table 5.4

Table 5.3. Reductions in Life-Cycle Costs

Case	Investment ($)	Investment/APUC	Reliability improvement (%)*	Cumulative costs from simulation (current $)	Savings ($)	Savings/base cost (%)
6	—	0	0	1,398,720,000	—	0
7	5,000,000	20	150	707,848,000	690,872,000	49.39
8	7,500,000	30	200	632,752,000	765,968,000	54.76
9	10,000,000	40	225	605,767,000	792,953,000	56.69

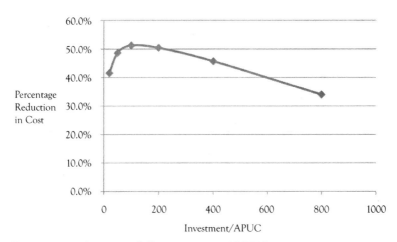

Figure 5.36. Constant dollar investment/APUC vs. percentage reduction in costs.

presents the impacts of improved reliability and failure-rate reductions on aircraft availability and readiness. Failure-rate reductions lower the average monthly removals and lead to increased annual aircraft-availability hours. In this analysis, it is assumed a part in repair would ground a helicopter for 3 days (72 hours). The table presents the annual additional hours of availability that arise from the improvements in reliability assumed in cases 6 to 9. As may be seen, the investments not only yield large savings in expenditures but also provide thousands of additional hours of availability.

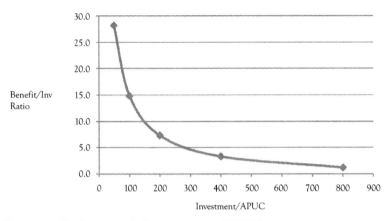

Figure 5.37. Constant dollar investment/APUC vs. return on investment.

Table 5.4. Impacts on Aircraft Availability and Readiness

Case	Failure rate reduction (failure rate per flight hour; %)	Average monthly demands	Unavailable hours per year*	Unavailable hours reduction (%)	Annual reduction in aircraft impacted	Annual additional available hours
6	—	14.0	12,096	—	—	—
7	60.0	7.4	6394	47.1	79	5702
8	66.7	6.7	5757	52.4	88	6339
9	69.2	6.4	5519	54.4	91	6577

Sensitivity Analysis

A sensitivity analysis was performed to examine the impacts of monthly demand rates and APUC on savings and return on investment. In the sensitivity analysis, all cases assume a 150% improvement in reliability. From the empirical relationship in Figure 5.1, this means an investment-to-APUC ratio of 20. Thus, for a part costing $250,000, the investment required is $5 million. For the part costing $500,000, the investment required is $10 million. As may be seen in Figure 5.38, the payback period in years (breakeven point) is achieved more quickly for a part with higher

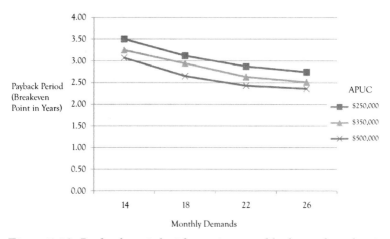

Figure 5.38. Payback period with varying monthly demands and unit costs.

demands because of the greater savings for high-volume parts. In addition, more expensive parts also exhibit faster paybacks than less expensive parts, again because of the greater savings. Figure 5.39 illustrates the cumulative savings for cases with higher demand rates and higher unit costs. Again, the greatest amount of cumulative savings is gained through helicopter parts with higher monthly demand and higher unit cost, as both variables directly impact cumulative savings over a system's useful life.

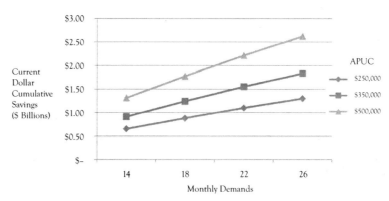

Figure 5.39. Cumulative savings with varying demands and unit costs.

Conclusions

"Doing more with less" has become a long-running and recurring theme across the globe. This challenge is especially acute for the U.S. Department of Defense and the branches of the armed services where demands are great and budgets are tight. Because typically the costs to operate, maintain, and dispose of a weapon system account for about 72% of the total cost of ownership, much effort has focused on these expenditures. Long-term costs incurred in maintenance are subject to increased focus. Affordability is now a key metric. Improvements in reliability have multiple cost-saving impacts, such as fewer parts to buy and overhaul, smaller inventories of replacement parts, fewer inspections, reduced maintenance hours and down time, and reduced transportation costs to ship replacement parts. Because of the complexities of the supply chain and procurement processes, financial evaluation of reliability investment is very difficult. The requirements-determination process, long production lead times, and target inventories must also be considered. An aviation supply chain system-dynamics model has been developed to enable evaluation of alternative cases in which investments are made to improve reliability, lower total demands, and reduce spending on new procurement and overhaul over the life cycle. It is shown that the payback potential of an investment depends on annual demand for the part, cost of the part, percentage improvement in reliability achieved, and any increase in cost of the part due to redesign. The analysis shows that returns can be high and payback periods can be fast, particularly for investments to improve reliability of items with high demand and high cost. Moreover, the simulation results indicate an investment "sweet spot" may exist in a range for the ratio of investment/product cost between 50 and 100. In this range, the percentage reduction in cost is maximized. The research also indicates that close coordination is needed between program management, procurement planning, and acquisition in order to fully realize savings. Ongoing research is developing reliability investment strategies and estimates for life-cycle costs under differing demand, manufacturing, and overhaul scenarios.

CHAPTER 6

The Role of Overhaul in Reducing Life-Cycle Costs and Maximizing the Return on Investments to Improve Reliability

Introduction

Maintaining aircraft in a high state of readiness requires a nonstop flow of spare parts. Almost every part on an aircraft will be replaced, repaired, and ultimately scrapped at some point in time. When parts must be removed, there are two primary sources for replacement parts: new parts from procurement and repaired parts coming from overhaul. The costs associated with the acquisition, overhaul, transportation, and labor to remove and install these parts are a significant part of a system's total operations and support (O&S) costs. Moreover, these O&S costs generally account for 70–80% of total life-cycle costs, and, as a result, much attention has been directed recently toward the reduction of O&S costs in Department of Defense (DoD) budgets.[1] One important strategy for reducing O&S costs is to improve reliability. A part with higher reliability is replaced less often, thus reducing maintenance labor and the required flow of new and repaired replacement parts. This reduction in the ongoing supply of replacement parts potentially, but not necessarily, reduces O&S costs. The overall cost impact depends on any increase in the cost of the new, improved part; the increase in reliability; and the demand level. Even if costs are reduced, an improvement in reliability may not be a sound business decision depending on the required investment. Business case analyses must answer the following questions: "What are the reductions in life-cycle costs arising from an investment in reliability improvement, and what are the return and payback times for the required investment?"

Previous efforts have investigated the likely payoffs arising from investments to improve reliability.[2] This research established a log-log linear relationship between the percentage of improvement in reliability and the ratio of the investment to the part cost. Killingsworth, Speciale, and Martin have taken a next step by estimating the cost reductions arising from the improved reliability and the returns on investment.[3] That research demonstrated that the returns generated by investments to improve reliability for aviation parts depended on the cost of the part, the flight hours per month, and the investment level. This prior research assumed that in the overhaul process, the removed parts could be transformed into the new design with improved reliability. This transformation, however, may not always be possible. There are three basic feasible scenarios regarding the old parts and overhaul:

1. Older parts can be transformed during the overhaul process into the new design with improved reliability. Thus both the new parts coming from acquisition and the parts coming from overhaul now possess the improved reliability. This was the assumption in the prior research.

2. The older parts cannot be transformed into the new parts, but there is either insufficient production capacity or insufficient funding to provide for all new parts. As a result, the old parts go through overhaul and are reissued but with the old level of reliability.

3. The older parts cannot be transformed into the new parts, but there is sufficient funding and production capacity for new parts to make up for the lost overhaul source. In this case, all old parts are scrapped. As a result, all parts being issued are new and possess higher reliability.

The objective of this research is to investigate the impacts of these three alternative overhaul scenarios on the returns generated by investments in reliability improvements. As noted, many factors affect the potential return: the cost of the new part, cost of the overhaul, operating hours, improvement in reliability, increase in cost arising from the improvement, and the investment being made. Moreover, since most aviation-system life spans can exceed 2 decades, the analysis must address the dynamics of the supply system over an extended time period. The analysis must capture the interplay of the many factors over time.

The intent of this system dynamics effort is to analyze the importance of overhaul (maintenance and repair) over the life span of an aviation system. Incorporating overhaul, total life-cycle costs, and improvements in reliability within a supply chain, a system dynamics model can capture both the multitude of variables and the dynamics of time. By using appropriate discount and inflation rates, cumulative and annual costs are measured in relation to investment amounts to weigh the overall benefits for reliability improvement and total overhaul costs within the government supply chain. By modeling the three specific overhaul scenarios for aviation parts in the supply chain over the system's life span, total costs (both constant and current dollars), benefit investment ratios, and payback periods can be determined for comparison.

Model Description

An overview of the supply chain for high-value aviation parts is shown in Figure 6.1. This diagram illustrates the flow of parts from new production and overhaul to the final customer. Also shown is the reverse logistics path in which removed parts may be returned to the overhaul facility for repair. The overall supply chain process is managed in a feedback form by the government's ordering or requirements-determination process.[4] These algorithms are typically embedded in a computerized process utilized by item managers, such as the U.S. Army's Supply Control Study. Based on the calculated recommendations, repair action or procurement action will be initiated. This process, or something similar, is used by most government and defense supply chains for high-value parts.[5]

By monitoring levels of inventory, due-ins, due-outs, and historical demand levels, the ordering process determines the recommended number of buys and repairs. The supply of parts comes from three possible sources: production of new items, commercial overhaul of worn or damaged parts, and government overhaul of worn or damaged parts. Once the production or overhaul process is completed, parts are transferred to

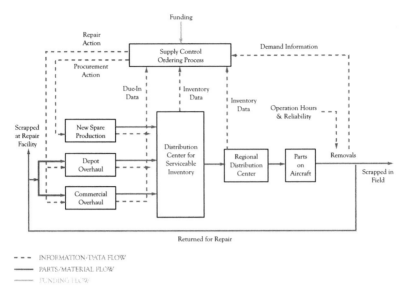

Figure 6.1. Overview of supply chain model.

a central distribution inventory. Geographical regions have an inventory of key spare parts, and these inventories are replenished from the central distribution inventory. The demand for a part is driven by the total number of installed parts, the monthly operating hours, and the failure rate per part per operating hour, sometimes expressed as a mean time between failures (MTBF). Removed parts that are excessively damaged and deemed unfit for repair may be scrapped in the field and not returned. Most high-dollar parts, however, are returned to a maintenance depot for evaluation. Those parts not scrapped upon evaluation will then be sent to either a government or a commercial overhaul facility. Parts coming from both new production and overhaul are delivered to the central inventory and are then available for shipment to the regional inventory centers.

The primary external drivers for the financial and supply chain model are listed in Figure 6.2. The MTBF is an engineering measure that specifies the amount of time (measured in hours) the part can be in operation before it is expected to fail. For this model, the initially assumed MBTF is 1390 hours. This number is increased to examine those cases with improved reliability. The monthly flying hours specifies the hours the aircraft and associated part are assumed to operate per month. For this analysis, 14 flying hours per month are assumed. The number of aircraft

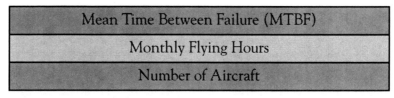

Mean Time Between Failure (MTBF)
Monthly Flying Hours
Number of Aircraft

Figure 6.2. Primary demand drivers for supply chain and financial model.

in this case is 463, and there are three installed parts of interest on each aircraft. There are thus 19,446 total monthly operating hours for the part of interest (14 flight hours per month × 463 aircraft × 3 installed parts per aircraft). With 1390 hours between failures, the total average failures per month is 14. This is the basic demand level and the number of removals each month.

The key assumed parameters within the model are presented in Figure 6.3. Before the production/repair process begins, contracts must be approved at various levels within the government; this elapsed time is known as administrative lead time (ALT) and typically ranges from a few weeks to 6 months. For this model, ALT is assumed to be 1 month. After contracts are in place, the repair or production process begins. The elapsed time between the contract(s) approval and part delivery to the government is called either the repair lead time (RLT) or production lead time (PLT). For this model, an 11-month RLT and 22-month PLT are assumed. The cost of a new part and cost of an overhauled part are the cost of a new part through procurement and the cost of a part repaired through overhaul, respectively. For this model it is assumed the cost of a new part is $250,000 and for a repaired part is $187,500. The inflation

Administrative Lead Time (ALT)	Inflation Rate
Repair Lead Time (RLT)	Discount Rate
Production Lead Time (PLT)	Scrap Rate in Field
Cost of New Part	Scrap Rate at Depot
Cost of Overhauled Part	

Figure 6.3. Important parameters for supply chain and financial model.

rate allows for forecasted growth in the price of all future expenditures. This model assumes a 6% inflation rate. The discount rate allows for analysis of a present value of expected costs within the simulation. Simply, this measure calculates the present value of total costs to be incurred in the future. A discount rate of 4% is used in this model. The scrap rate in the field is the percentage of parts scrapped in the field and deemed unserviceable and unable to be repaired. For scenarios 1 and 2, the scrap rate in the field is 15%. For scenario 3, the scrap rate in the field is 100%, meaning no parts are returned to the depot for evaluation. The scrap rate at the depot is the percentage of parts scrapped at the depot facility following evaluation. For scenarios 1 and 2, this number is 35%. As noted, in scenario 3, no parts are returned for evaluation at the depot.

The intent of this research is to determine how investments made in the supply chain for improved reliability reduce total life-cycle costs under alternative overhaul scenarios. It is assumed in the model that the investment occurs over a 3-year period that includes design, manufacturing, test, and certification. Shorter or longer investment periods are easily included and examined in the model structure.

The investment in reliability impacts the spending amounts for each year after the new, improved part is introduced, depending on the degree of reliability improvement for the part and any changes in the unit cost of the part. It may very well be the case that the improved part will have a higher production cost, and the model enables the investigation of trade-off between improved reliability, higher unit cost, and reduced demand.

The three overhaul scenarios are described in greater detail:

1. In this first scenario, the older parts that are removed are transformed during the overhaul process into the new design with improved reliability. Thus new parts coming from acquisition and also parts coming from overhaul now possess the improved reliability. This was the assumption in the prior research effort. For this scenario, the scrap rate in the field is 15%, and the scrap rate at the depot facility is 35%. Figure 6.4 shows an overview of the model structure for this scenario.

2. In the second scenario, the older parts that are removed from the aircraft cannot be transformed in overhaul to the new design with higher reliability. These older design parts undergo overhaul but are

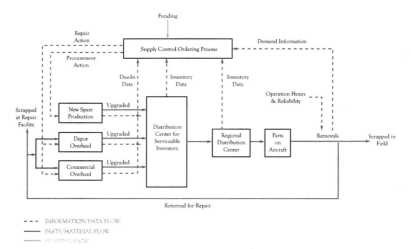

Figure 6.4. Overview of model structure for scenario 1: Reliability of older parts upgraded during the overhaul process.

returned to the supply system with the prior reliability levels. Thus the population is a renewing mix of new and old designs. The newly procured parts operate at the new and improved reliability levels, but the old, refurbished parts will remain in operation at original reliability levels. In this case, it takes much longer to reach overall improved reliability levels and reduced demands. For this scenario the scrap rate in the field is 15% and the scrap rate at the depot facility is 35%. Prior research has not examined this scenario. Figure 6.5 presents an overview of the model for this scenario.

3. In the third scenario, the older parts cannot be transformed into the new, improved reliability part. This is similar to the assumption in scenario 2. It is assumed in this scenario, however, that there is sufficient funding and production capacity for an increase in the production rate of new parts to make up for the overhaul. In this case, all old parts are scrapped. A key assumption for this case is that the supply chain has the capacity and resources to manufacture the new parts fast enough to fill all orders and overcome the lack of overhaul supply. For this scenario the scrap rate in the field is 100%, as all parts removed from the aircraft will be replaced with only newly procured parts. Figure 6.6 presents the model overview for this case in which there is no reverse logistics of old parts following the introduction of the new part. Prior research has not examined this scenario.

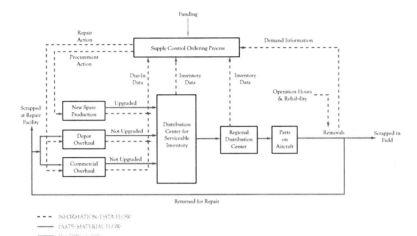

Figure 6.5. Overview of model structure for scenario 2: Reliability of older parts not upgraded during the overhaul process.

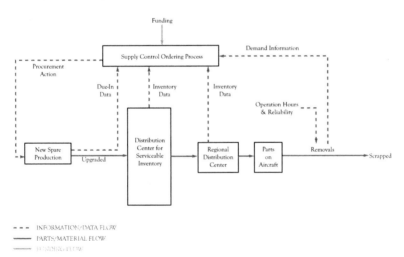

Figure 6.6. Overview of model structure for scenario 3: Only new parts are issued, no overhaul process after introduction of improved, more reliable new part.

Financial Analysis and Supply Chain Behavior

Because of the strong tie between reliability and sustainment costs, Charles E. McQueary, Director, Operational Test and Evaluation, Office of the Secretary of Defense, sponsored research to investigate the empirical relationships between reliability investments, improvements in reliability,

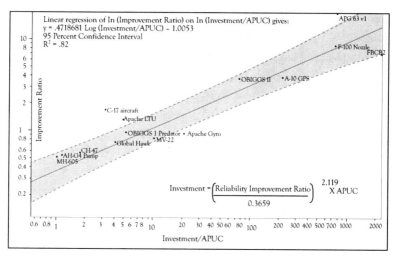

Figure 6.7. Empirical relationship between reliability improvements and reliability investments.

and life-cycle support costs. In this research, a preliminary relationship between investment in reliability (normalized by average production unit cost) and achieved reliability improvement was developed. This relationship is presented in Figure 6.7 and is taken from a presentation delivered by McQueary.

As an illustrative data point on the graph of Figure 6.7, the research determined that the Predator program invested a total cumulative amount of $39.1 million in reliability investments over a 9-year period. The ratio of this investment to the average production unit cost (APUC) of $4.2 million is 9.3 and is the value of the x-axis for the Predator data point. The research also determined that the overall failure rate of the Predator was reduced by 48.1%, resulting in an overall improvement in the MTBF from 40 hours in fiscal year (FY)98 to 77 hours in FY06, or a 92.5% improvement in reliability. This is the y-axis point for the Predator. The other data points on this graph reflect the results of similar analysis.

For the analysis presented in this research, cases are evaluated for investment/APUC ratios of 20 (case 1), 30 (case 2), and 40 (case 3). For a part costing $250,000, these cases require investments of $5 million, $7.5 million, and $10 million. These scenarios had corresponding reliability improvement ratios of 1.5, 2.0, and 2.25, respectively. The improvement ratios of 1.5 (150%), 2.0 (200%), and 2.25 (225%) may be viewed as generating percentage reductions in failure rate per flight hour of 60% (case 1), 66.7% (case 2), and 69.2% (case 3). These three cases are used in analysis of the three overhaul scenarios.

For each scenario, a base case projection is compared to several alternative cases that include reductions in failure rate per flight hour of 60.0%, 66.7%, and 69.2%. Each case has an associated investment amount for its specific improvement in reliability. Annual spending is used to determine the payback ratio in years (i.e., breakeven) and the total benefit for the predetermined investment amount. In addition, for each case, the total annual costs and benefit per defined investment are determined. These results indicate those investment amounts that are most appropriate for achieving the greatest cost savings and total benefit.

Overhaul Scenario 1: Old Parts Undergo Overhaul, Are Upgraded in Overhaul, and Are Reissued with New, Improved Level of Reliability

For scenario 1, overhauled parts are capable of being upgraded to the new level of improved reliability. Once the improved part becomes available at the beginning of year 4, all parts being issued have improved reliability. For this scenario, three cases of improved reliability are examined. Figures 6.8 to 6.11 present the simulation results for the case with the greatest reliability improvement, a 69.2% reduction in failures per flight hour. Figure 6.8 presents the recurring monthly demands for this case. With constant flight hours, demand is constant at 14 per month until the new parts begin to be introduced. Each time an older part is removed, a part with improved reliability is installed, and, as a result, the overall average mean time between failures begins to decline, reflecting the mix of new and old parts. After approximately 8 years, all the parts are the improved parts with higher reliabillity, and demand has dropped to a new steady level. Since parts are lasting longer, fewer parts are demanded. Figure 6.9 illustrates that when the total net assets drop below the procurement reorder point, a procurement action ordering new parts is initiated. The total net assets are calculated by summing the available wholesale inventories and the items due in from procurement and repair processes, and subtracting the number of items due out. As may be seen in Figure 6.9, there is an 8-year period where total net assets exceed the reorder point. This creates an 8-year period where no parts are ordered through new

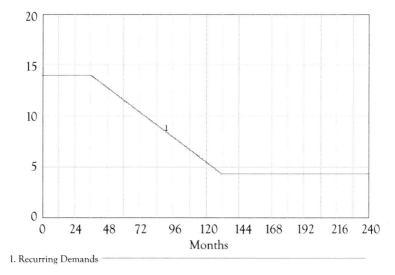

1. Recurring Demands

Figure 6.8. Recurring demands for scenario 1.

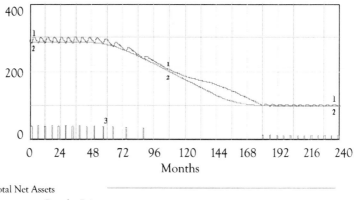

1. Total Net Assets
2. Procurement Reorder Point
3. Procurement Action

Figure 6.9. Procurement action for scenario 1.

procurement. This period of time with no new orders can be explained by reviewing the graph of inventories presented in Figure 6.11. The growth in inventories is largely the result of long time lags in the system. First, forecast demands used to calculate the reorder point are often based on a 2-year rolling average of demand. Thus, as the improved parts begin to reduce demand, that reduction is only slowly taken into account in the rolling average and the forecast. Second, the production lead time is 2

1. Total Overhaul Completion Rate
2. New Procurement Completion Rate

Figure 6.10. Overhaul and new procurement production completion rates.

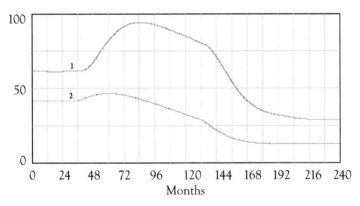

1. Serviceable Inventory
2. Available Inventory at Regions

Figure 6.11. Inventories for scenario 1.

years, so a significant pipeline of production work in progress exists. This pipeline empties into the supply system at the same time that demand is falling and, as a result, inventories increase. With the growth in inventories, new production is essentially halted for several years and only repaired parts are needed to sustain operations. Figure 6.10 illustrates the completion rates for overhaul and new procurement. Both completion rates decline once the reliability-improved parts are introduced. The halt in new production is not a good thing and, in fact, could be quite troublesome. The industrial base for many defense aviation parts is quite small, and this type of gap could well lead to a loss of suppliers. Integrated planning and careful forecasting of inventories could prevent the excess supply and the cutback in orders.

Figure 6.12 presents the financial results for scenario 1. This chart presents the current-dollar annual expenditures for the base case and three cases with improved reliability. Note that the spend column for each case includes the investment being made over the first 3 years in which the new part is developed. Thus, for case 1, the negative savings (expressed in current dollars) of $1.6 million, $1.8 million, and $1.8 million in the first three years are equal to the initial investment amount of $5 million. Once the improved part is introduced at the beginning of year 4, positive annual savings begin to accrue. For cases 1, 2, and 3, the cumulative lifetime savings are $655.6 million, $725.7 million, and $752.0 million, respectively. It is important to note that these large savings are arising from an investment in reliability for a single part with a monthly demand of 14 and a cost of $250,000 per unit. This indicates the very large potential in life-cycle savings that improved reliability makes possible. All the breakeven payback points are between 3 and 3.4 years, a fairly rapid payoff for the investments. However, as may be seen in the lower section of Figure 6.12, the ratio of benefits to investment has a much broader range, going from 131 for case 1 to 97 for case 2, and dropping to 75 for case 3 with the highest investment of $10 million. This clearly indicates the very real potential for diminishing returns on higher levels of investment.

It is important to note that in the three cases of improved reliability previously discussed, the cost of the improved part with higher reliability remains at $250,000. Killingsworth, Speciale, and Martin have examined the impacts on the financial benefits of increases in part cost due to the new design.[6] This analysis showed that such a cost increase would reduce the savings and the benefit-to-investment ratio, but under reasonable assumptions for cost increase, the financial benefits remained very attractive.

Current Dollars Annual Spending Amounts ($Millions)*							
	Percent Reduction in Failure Rate Per Flight Hour						
Year	Base Spend 0%	Case 1 Spend 60%	Case 1 Savings	Case 2 Spend 66.7%	Case 2 Savings	Case 3 Spend 69.2%	Case 3 Savings
1	$36.2	$37.8	-$1.6	$38.7	-$2.5	$39.5	-$3.3
2	$38.3	$40.1	-$1.8	$41.0	-$2.7	$41.9	-$3.6
3	$40.9	$42.7	-$1.8	$43.7	-$2.8	$44.6	-$3.7
4	$43.4	$43.4	$0.0	$43.4	$0.0	$43.4	$0.0
5	$46.0	$45.9	$0.1	$45.9	$0.1	$45.9	$0.1
6	$48.8	$44.7	$4.1	$44.1	$4.7	$43.9	$4.9
7	$51.8	$40.5	$11.3	$39.2	$12.6	$38.7	$13.1
8	$55.1	$36.1	$19.0	$34.1	$21.0	$33.4	$21.7
9	$58.5	$32.5	$26.0	$28.2	$30.3	$28.7	$29.8
10	$62.1	$29.1	$33.0	$25.4	$36.7	$24.2	$37.9
11	$65.9	$25.9	$40.0	$21.1	$44.8	$19.9	$46.0
12	$70.0	$22.2	$47.8	$17.0	$53.0	$15.4	$54.6
13	$74.3	$18.8	$55.5	$13.6	$60.7	$11.6	$62.7
14	$78.9	$20.7	$58.2	$15.3	$63.6	$13.3	$65.6
15	$83.8	$26.3	$57.5	$19.7	$64.1	$17.7	$66.1
16	$89.0	$32.0	$57.0	$24.3	$64.7	$21.6	$67.4
17	$94.5	$36.3	$58.2	$29.2	$65.3	$25.2	$69.3
18	$100.3	$39.3	$61.0	$32.5	$67.8	$29.2	$71.1
19	$106.5	$42.4	$64.1	$35.3	$71.2	$32.3	$74.2
20	$113.1	$45.1	$68.0	$40.0	$73.1	$35.0	$78.1
Cumulative	$1,357.4	$701.8	$655.6	$631.7	$725.7	$605.4	$752.0
Investment Over 3-Year Period (Years 1–3)**							
Case 1 $5 Million	Breakeven (Years)	3.08					
Case 2 $7.5 Million	Breakeven (Years)			3.21			
Case 3 $10 Million	Breakeven (Years)					3.38	
Ratio of Benefits to Investment***							
Case 1 $5 Million		131.0					
Case 2 $7.5 Million				96.8			
Case 3 $10 Million						75.2	

*Annual spending amounts include investment spending during first three years
**Breakeven period is the time required to recapture the investment through savings after the investment period
***Benefits are the total cumulative savings

Figure 6.12. Financial results for scenario 1: Cases base, 1, 2, and 3.

Overhaul Scenario 2: Old Parts Undergo Overhaul But Are Not Upgraded in Overhaul and Are Reissued with Old Reliability

For scenario 2, it is assumed that the overhaul process cannot upgrade older parts to perform at the same reliability levels as the new parts. It is assumed, moreover, that there is neither the funding nor the production capacity to do away with overhaul and supply only new parts. As a consequence, at the beginning of year 4, new parts with improved reliability are being introduced into the system along with older parts coming from overhaul, which have the historical reliability level. Figures 6.13 to 6.16 present the simulation results for this overhaul scenario. Figure 6.13 illustrates the level of recurring demands over time. Significantly different from scenario 1, the level of recurring demands requires more than 16 years to reach the new lower level. This is because, in scenario 1, all parts used for replacements had the new higher level of reliability. In contrast, in scenario 2, many of the parts being used have the older level of reliability. It thus takes longer for the changeover in the population. Figure 6.14 presents the procurement actions over time. As the new parts are introduced, the time between orders lengthens, and the order size becomes somewhat smaller. Similar to scenario 1, a lower total level of net assets

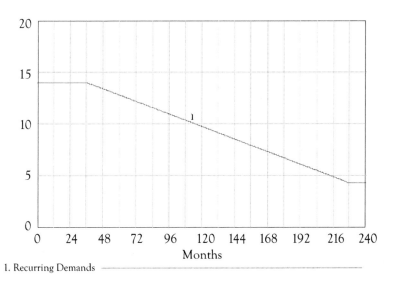

1. Recurring Demands

Figure 6.13. Recurring demands for scenario 2.

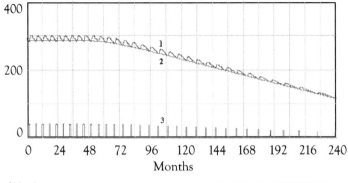

1. Total Net Assets
2. Procurement Reorder Point
3. Procurement Action

Figure 6.14. Procurement action for scenario 2.

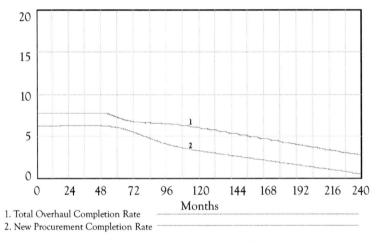

1. Total Overhaul Completion Rate
2. New Procurement Completion Rate

Figure 6.15. Overhaul and new procurement production completion rates.

is required over time, as more newly improved parts enter the supply chain and demand drops. Figure 6.15 illustrates the total overhaul and new procurement completion rates. For this scenario, both completion rates decline correspondingly once the new parts are introduced. Figure 6.16 shows that inventory levels increase upon the introduction of the reliability-improved parts and then decline for the remainder of the simulation. It is important to note that for this case, with demand falling much more slowly, the inventories do not grow to the same extent as

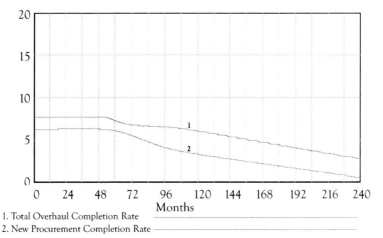

1. Total Overhaul Completion Rate
2. New Procurement Completion Rate

Figure 6.16. Inventories for scenario 2.

in scenario 1 and there is no period without orders for new parts as was seen in scenario 1. This is a positive development for the stability of the supplier base.

Figure 6.17 presents the financial results for scenario 2 including the base case and reliability-improvement cases 1, 2, and 3. Note that the reliability improvements and the investments are the same as in scenario 1, yet total cumulative savings are much lower, the payback years are higher, and the benefit-to-investment ratio is lower for all three cases compared to scenario 1. Recall that in scenario 1, all older parts were upgraded to the higher reliability design during the overhaul process. This means that starting in year 4 of scenario 1, all parts being supplied have higher reliability, and demand drops fairly quickly over a period of 8 years. In contrast, in scenario 2, the older parts cannot be upgraded and after overhaul are returned to service with the lower reliability. As a result, turnover of parts occurs more slowly and demand does not drop quickly, requiring approximately 16 years to reach the new lower level. The resulting consequence is that savings do not accrue as rapidly, and this scenario has lower financial returns and is not as attractive as scenario 1.

Current Dollars Annual Spending Amounts ($Millions)*							
	Percent Reduction in Failure Rate Per Flight Hour						
Year	Base Spend 0%	Case 1 Spend 60%	Case 1 Savings	Case 2 Spend 66.7%	Case 2 Savings	Case 3 Spend 69.2%	Case 3 Savings
1	$36.2	$37.8	-$1.6	$38.7	-$2.5	$39.5	-$3.3
2	$38.3	$40.1	-$1.8	$41.0	-$2.7	$41.9	-$3.6
3	$40.9	$42.7	-$1.8	$43.7	-$2.8	$44.6	-$3.7
4	$43.4	$43.4	$0.0	$43.4	$0.0	$43.4	$0.0
5	$46.0	$46.0	$0.0	$46.0	$0.0	$46.0	$0.0
6	$48.8	$47.0	$1.8	$46.7	$2.1	$46.6	$2.2
7	$51.8	$46.2	$5.6	$45.6	$6.2	$45.3	$6.5
8	$55.1	$45.7	$9.4	$44.7	$10.4	$44.3	$10.8
9	$58.5	$45.6	$12.9	$44.1	$14.4	$43.5	$15.0
10	$62.1	$45.7	$16.4	$43.7	$18.4	$43.0	$19.1
11	$65.9	$45.8	$20.1	$43.6	$22.3	$42.9	$23.0
12	$70.0	$46.0	$24.0	$43.6	$26.4	$42.6	$27.4
13	$74.3	$46.3	$28.0	$42.9	$31.4	$41.6	$32.7
14	$78.9	$46.1	$32.8	$42.3	$36.6	$41.2	$37.7
15	$83.8	$45.6	$38.2	$41.7	$42.1	$39.8	$44.0
16	$89.0	$45.4	$43.6	$40.1	$48.9	$38.6	$50.4
17	$94.5	$44.5	$50.0	$39.1	$55.4	$36.8	$57.7
18	$100.3	$43.3	$57.0	$37.2	$63.1	$34.6	$65.7
19	$106.5	$42.3	$64.2	$34.9	$71.6	$32.3	$74.2
20	$113.1	$40.5	$72.6	$32.5	$80.6	$29.4	$83.7
Cumulative	$1,357.4	$886.0	$471.4	$835.5	$521.9	$817.9	$539.5
Investment Over 3-Year Period (Years 1–3)**							
Case 1 $5 Million	Breakeven (Years)	3.57					
Case 2 $7.5 Million	Breakeven (Years)			3.87			
Case 3 $10 Million	Breakeven (Years)					4.12	
Ratio of Benefits to Investment***							
Case 1 $5 Million		94.3					
Case 2 $7.5 Million				69.6			
Case 3 $10 Million						54.0	

*Annual spending amounts include investment spending during first three years

**Breakeven period is the time required to recapture the investment through savings after the investment period

***Benefits are the total cumulative savings

Figure 6.17. Financial results for scenario 2: Cases base, 1, 2, and 3.

Overhaul Scenario 3: All Old Parts Are Scrapped and Do Not Undergo Overhaul; New Production Ramps up to Overcome Loss of Overhaul Supply Stream

In scenario 3, it is assumed that all the removed parts with the old design are scrapped and do not undergo overhaul. A highly important assumption for this scenario is that funding and production capacity are sufficient to do away with the overhaul of the older design part. Thus, at the beginning of year 4, only parts from new procurement are introduced as replacements in the system. Over time, as these new parts are removed, they are then returned for overhaul and maintain the new higher reliability levels. However, it takes some time for those parts to begin appearing in the reverse logistics flow. Figures 6.18 to 6.21 present the simulation results for scenario 3. Figure 6.18 illustrates the recurring demands level over time. Similar to scenario 1, once the improved-reliability parts are introduced, the recurring demands decline over approximately 8 years as the part mix goes from all older parts to all newly designed parts. The overall dynamics of this scenario are more complex than in the first two scenarios. Figure 6.19 shows a decline in the procurement reorder point similar to that seen in scenario 1. This decline in the "target" reorder point is due to the reduced demands arising from the more rapid introduction of improved parts than in scenario 2. Figures 6.19 and 6.20 show

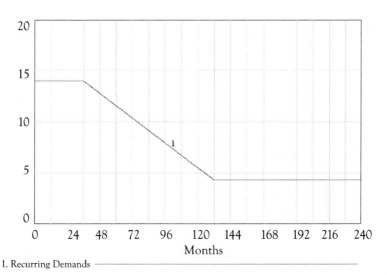

1. Recurring Demands

Figure 6.18. Recurring demands for scenario 3.

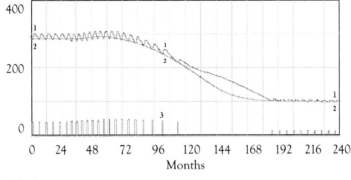

1. Total Net Assets
2. Procurement Reorder Point
3. Procurement Action

Figure 6.19. Procurement actions for scenario 3.

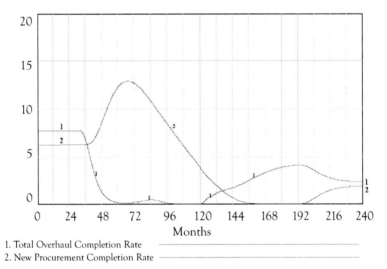

1. Total Overhaul Completion Rate
2. New Procurement Completion Rate

Figure 6.20. Overhaul and new procurement production completion rates.

a substantial growth in new procurement since overhaul parts are not used for some period of time. As in scenario 1, the pipeline of improved parts (ordered 2 years previously in an era of higher demand) enters the supply system as demand is falling. As a result, as may be seen in Figure 6.21, inventories build up. This leads then to a period of time with no orders for new parts. On the other hand, the total overhaul completion

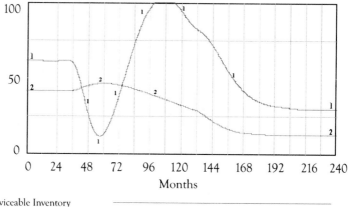

1. Serviceable Inventory
2. Available Inventory at Regions

Figure 6.21. Inventories for scenario 3.

rate drops off completely for a few years because the older parts are not undergoing overhaul. After roughly 6 years, a sufficient number of new parts are being returned for overhaul, and that overhaul program largely supports the demands for a period of time. Note in Figure 6.21 that the serviceable inventory level drops significantly at the beginning of year 4 because all the old design parts are scrapped, and production of new parts has not ramped up as quickly. Because only newly improved parts are entering the supply chain, there is a lag before the serviceable inventory begins to rise. The long lead times and lag periods account for the difficulty in planning and the complex dynamics.

Figure 6.22 presents the financial results for scenario 3 including the base case and reliability-improvement cases 1, 2, and 3. Note that the benefit-to-investment ratio is similar to scenario 1 but much better than scenario 2. Recall that in scenario 1, all older parts were upgraded to the higher reliability design during the overhaul process. This means that starting in year 4 of scenario 1, all parts being supplied have higher reliability, and demand drops fairly quickly over a period of 8 years. In scenario 3, all new parts are being introduced with a corresponding rapid drop in demand. The key difference between scenarios 1 and 3 is the higher cost of a new part compared to the cost of an overhauled part. This difference creates slightly lower savings for scenario 3. Both scenarios 1 and 3 have greater returns than scenario 2, with the slow introduction of parts with improved reliability.

Current Dollars Annual Spending Amounts ($Millions)*							
Percent Reduction in Failure Rate Per Flight Hour							
Year	Base Spend 0%	Case 1 Spend 60%	Case 1 Savings	Case 2 Spend 66.7%	Case 2 Savings	Case 3 Spend 69.2%	Case 3 Savings
1	$36.2	$37.8	–$1.6	$38.7	–$2.5	$39.5	–$3.3
2	$38.3	$40.1	–$1.8	$41.0	–$2.7	$41.9	–$3.6
3	$40.9	$42.7	–$1.8	$43.7	–$2.8	$44.6	–$3.7
4	$40.9	$40.9	$0.0	$40.9	$0.0	$40.9	$0.0
5	$37.6	$37.5	$0.1	$37.5	$0.1	$37.5	$0.1
6	$53.0	$51.1	$1.9	$50.9	$2.1	$50.8	$2.2
7	$63.2	$56.2	$7.0	$55.2	$8.0	$54.9	$8.3
8	$71.2	$53.6	$17.6	$51.5	$19.7	$50.7	$20.5
9	$78.3	$45.6	$32.7	$42.2	$36.1	$41.0	$37.3
10	$77.3	$36.4	$40.9	$32.4	$44.9	$30.9	$46.4
11	$74.5	$27.7	$46.8	$22.5	$52.0	$20.5	$54.0
12	$75.9	$24.6	$51.3	$18.5	$57.4	$16.3	$59.6
13	$77.3	$19.8	$57.5	$13.9	$63.4	$12.0	$65.3
14	$79.4	$20.6	$58.8	$15.1	$64.3	$13.2	$66.2
15	$82.5	$25.1	$57.4	$19.6	$62.9	$17.6	$64.9
16	$86.3	$30.7	$55.6	$23.6	$62.7	$21.6	$64.7
17	$92.8	$35.9	$56.9	$27.9	$64.9	$24.5	$68.3
18	$98.5	$39.3	$59.2	$32.1	$66.4	$28.3	$70.2
19	$104.8	$42.2	$62.6	$35.3	$69.5	$32.2	$72.6
20	$112.0	$45.0	$67.0	$37.6	$74.4	$34.8	$77.2
Cumulative	$1420.9	$752.8	$668.1	$680.1	$740.8	$653.7	$767.2
Investment Over 3-Year Period (Years 1–3)**							
Case 1 $5 Million	Breakeven (Years)	3.43					
Case 2 $7.5 Million	Breakeven (Years)			3.66			
Case 3 $10 Million	Breakeven (Years)					3.93	
Ratio of Benefits to Investment***							
Case 1 $5 Million		133.6					
Case 2 $7.5 Million				98.8			
Case 3 $10 Million						76.7	

*Annual spending amounts include investment spending during first three years
**Breakeven period is the time required to recapture the investment through savings after the investment period
***Benefits are the total cumulative savings

Figure 6.22. Financial results for scenario 3: Cases base, 1, 2, and 3.

Sensitivity and Comparative Analysis

Figure 6.7 presented an empirically derived relationship between percentage improvement in reliability and the ratio of investment to part cost. As indicated earlier, this relationship was used to determine the reliability impacts on a part costing $250,000 arising from investments of $5 million, $7.5 million, and $10 million to improve reliability. From Figure 6.7, for a part costing $250,000, these investments would lead to reliability improvements of 150%, 200%, and 225%. These improvement levels were the alternative cases used for the three overhaul scenarios. Figures 6.23 to 6.25 present reduction in life-cycle spending and the benefit-to-investment ratio for a wide range of investment ratios, going from 0 to 800—that is, an investment 800 times the cost of the product. Results are presented for the three overhaul scenarios. These charts present the investment ratios, the resultant reliability-improvement ratios, and from the simulation results, the total cumulative spending, the percentage reductions in life-cycle spending, and the benefit-(i.e., savings)-to-investment ratios for both constant and current dollars.

Investment/APUC	Reliability-improvement ratio*	Constant dollars			Current dollars		
		Total spending ($ millions)**	Percentage reduction in spending (%)***	Benefit/investment ratio****	Total spending ($ millions)	Percentage reduction in spending (%)	Benefit/investment ratio
0 (Base)	0.0	724	—	—	1357	—	—
20 (Case 1)	1.5	423	42	60.2	702	48	131.0
50	2.5	372	49	28.2	582	57	62.0
100	3.5	353	51	14.8	521	62	33.4
200	5.0	359	50	7.3	507	63	17.0
400	7.0	393	46	3.3	523	61	8.3
800	9.0	478	34	1.2	600	56	3.8

Figure 6.23. Scenario 1: Old parts undergo overhaul, are upgraded in overhaul, and are reissued with new, improved level of reliability.

Investment/APUC	Reliability-improvement ratio*	Constant dollars			Current dollars		
		Total spending ($ millions)**	Percentage reduction in spending (%)***	Benefit/investment ratio****	Total spending ($ millions)	Percentage reduction in spending (%)	Benefit/investment ratio
0 (Base)	0.0	724	—	—	1357	—	—
20 (Case 1)	1.5	516	29	41.6	886	35	94.2
50	2.5	483	33	19.3	798	41	44.7
100	3.5	474	35	10.0	757	44	24.0
200	5.0	484	33	4.8	750	45	12.1
400	7.0	521	28	2.0	772	43	5.9
800	9.0	610	16	0.6	855	37	2.5

Figure 6.24. Scenario 2: Old parts undergo overhaul but are not upgraded in overhaul and are reissued with old reliability.

The results in Figures 6.23 to 6.25 are presented as graphs in Figures 6.26 to 6.29. Figures 6.26 and 6.27 clearly show that the maximum percentage reduction in spending is achieved at an investment ratio of approximately 100. Below this level of investment, potential benefits are being left on the table. Above this ratio, diminishing returns are evident in that the higher and higher investments are not generating sufficient benefits to overcome the large investments. Figures 6.28 and 6.29 present the return on investment defined as the ratio of benefits (savings) to investment. As may be seen, these returns fall off sharply as the investment increases. Note that these are benefit ratios, not percentages, so that for an investment ratio of 100 the benefit ratio ranges between 10 and 15 (using constant dollars), for a return percentage of 1000% to 1500%. The returns are so substantial because 20-year life-cycle spending reductions are very large, ranging from $700 million to $900 million for a single part that costs $250,000. These results dramatically illustrate the benefits possible by improving reliability.

Investment/APUC	Reliability-improvement ratio*	Constant dollars			Current dollars		
		Total spending ($ millions)**	Percentage reduction in spending (%)***	Benefit/investment ratio****	Total spending ($ millions)	Percentage reduction in spending (%)	Benefit/investment ratio
0 (Base)	0.0	763	—	—	1421	—	—
20 (Case 1)	1.5	455	40	61.6	753	47	133.6
50	2.5	403	47	28.8	631	56	63.2
100	3.5	382	50	15.2	568	60	34.1
200	5.0	388	49	7.5	551	61	17.4
400	7.0	419	45	3.4	564	60	8.6
800	9.0	505	34	1.3	638	55	3.9

Figure 6.25. Scenario 3: All old parts are scrapped and do not undergo overhaul; new production ramps up to overcome loss of overhaul supply stream.

*Derived from Figure 6.7

**Investment amount included in total spend amount

***Calculated by dividing total benefit (savings) by base case total spend amount

****Calculated by dividing total benefit (savings) by investment amount

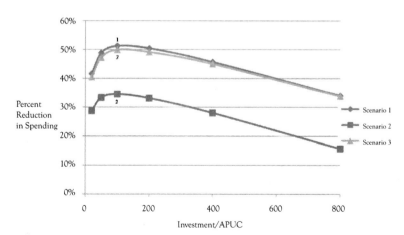

Figure 6.26. Constant dollars percentage reduction in spending as a function of investment in improved reliability.

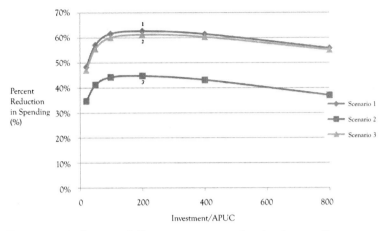

Figure 6.27. Current dollars percentage reduction in spending as a function of investment in improved reliability.

Note: Scenarios 1 and 3 overlap in Figure 6.27.

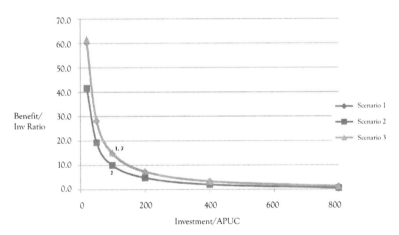

Figure 6.28. Constant dollars benefit/investment ratio as a function of investment in improved reliability.

Note: Scenarios 1 and 3 overlap in the figure above.

Conclusion

Maintaining aircraft in a high state of readiness requires a nonstop flow of spare parts. When parts must be removed, two primary sources for replacement parts exist: new parts from procurement and repaired parts

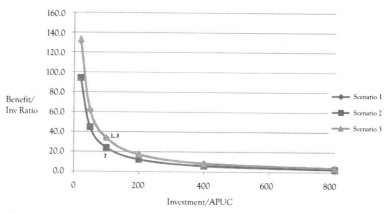

Figure 6.29. Current dollars benefit/investment ratio as a function of investment in improved reliability.

coming from overhaul. The costs associated with the acquisition, overhaul, transportation, and labor to remove and install these parts are a significant part of a system's total O&S costs. Moreover, these O&S costs generally account for 70% to 80% of total life-cycle costs, and, as a result, much attention has been directed recently toward the reduction of O&S costs in Defense budgets. One important approach for reducing O&S costs is to improve reliability. A part with higher reliability is replaced less often, thus reducing maintenance labor and the required flow of new and repaired replacement parts. This reduction in the ongoing supply of replacement parts potentially, but not necessarily, reduces O&S costs. The overall cost impact depends on any increase in the cost of the new, improved part; the increase in reliability; the demand level; and whether older parts can be transformed to the new, more reliable design through overhaul. Even if costs are reduced, an improvement in reliability may not be a sound business decision depending on the required investment. Business case analyses must answer these questions: What are the reductions in life-cycle costs arising from an investment in reliability improvement; what are the return and payback time for the required investment; and what role does overhaul play in determining life-cycle returns?

Three overhaul scenarios have been examined to evaluate the payback and returns generated by investments to improve the reliability of certain aviation parts. These scenarios are as follows:

1. Older parts can be transformed during the overhaul process into the new design with improved reliability. Thus both the new parts coming from acquisition and the parts coming from overhaul now possess the improved reliability.

2. The older parts cannot be transformed into the new parts, but there is either insufficient production capacity or funding to provide for all new parts. As a result, the old parts go through overhaul and are reissued but with the old level of reliability.

3. The older parts cannot be transformed into the new parts, but there is sufficient funding and production capacity for new parts to make up for the lost overhaul source. In this case, all old parts are scrapped. As a result, all parts being issued are new and possess higher reliability.

A system dynamics supply chain and financial model was developed to investigate these scenarios through simulation. This model incorporates the requirements-determination process that controls many government supply chains in a feedback fashion. The model shows that all three scenarios reduce total life-cycle costs and that these reductions can be very significant. The system dynamics supply chain and financial-simulation model demonstrate how these life-cycle cost reductions depend on the levels of reliability, investment amounts, and the role of overhaul.

The life-cycle simulations show that the financial results are somewhat similar for scenarios 1 and 3. These scenarios are similar because, after year 4, all parts being issued have the improved reliability. It must be noted that scenario 1 can be difficult to implement because it assumes the older parts can be upgraded to the new, improved reliability level during overhaul. If design changes are significant, then this may not be possible. Scenario 3 assumes that all older parts are scrapped and that production capacity can be increased to make up for the lost overhaul. Again, this scenario may be difficult to implement either because of funding limitations or because of the production constraints of the U.S. industrial base. In general, overhaul scenario 1 financially outperforms the other two scenarios, although scenario 3 is often very competitive. In scenario 3, since all parts being issued are newly procured parts, the annual spending amounts are higher, based on the original assumption that new parts are more expensive than repaired parts. Scenario 2 offers the least potential for cost savings since old parts emerge from overhaul with the old level of reliability. This delays both the realization of lower demands and the financial benefits. In scenarios 1 and 3, the changeover between old and new parts in the population requires about 8 years. In scenario 2, the changeover requires about 16 years since older parts are reissued from overhaul with the old reliability level.

Although all scenarios have relatively quick payback ratios, scenario 1 recaptures its investment the quickest. Since scenario 1 allows initial parts to be upgraded and returned for service at the new reliability level, fewer funds are used to buy solely new procured parts (scenario 3). This unique capability allows the overhaul process of scenario 1 to endure greater cost savings immediately after the investment period, as compared to scenario 3.

All scenarios illustrate that improvements in reliability can greatly reduce the total costs. However, it is noted that the possibility for cost reductions cannot continue to increase forever. Diminishing returns exist as the investment amount grows past a certain level. If the investment amount is too substantial, cost savings can still be achieved but not in the most efficient form. O&S costs may be greatly decreased in size, but excessive investment and production costs will counteract the main goal of reducing total life-cycle costs. The analysis shows clearly that the maximum percentage reduction in spending is achieved at an investment ratio of approximately 100. Below this level of investment, potential benefits are being left on the table. Above this ratio, diminishing returns are evident in that the higher and higher investments are not generating sufficient benefits to overcome the large investments. It is shown that returns fall off sharply as the investment increases. Note that these are benefit ratios, not percentages, so that for an investment ratio of 100 the benefit ratio ranges between 10 and 15 (using constant dollars) for a return percentage of 1000% to 1500%. The returns are so substantial because 20-year life-cycle spend reductions are very large, ranging from $700 million to $900 million for a single part that costs $250,000. These results dramatically illustrate the benefits possible by improving reliability and the important role that overhaul plays in achieving these benefits.

CHAPTER 7

Future Supply Chains and System Dynamics

Future supply chain discussions will be dominated by three overarching topics: greater complexity, increased velocity, and heightened volatility. These three factors are a dangerous and threatening mix. Complexity will continue to increase with the ongoing growth of the virtual enterprise— the hundreds, if not thousands, of companies that work together to produce and deliver a product or service. These complex distributed networks create heightened demands for supply chain coordination and collaboration. Increased velocity will be driven by the need for faster speed to market, shorter planning cycles, greater clock speeds for technology and, in many cases, ever shorter product life cycles. But the third factor truly multiplies the threats: in addition to greater complexity and increased velocity, supply chain executives will need to cope with heightened volatility due to greater variability in economic, financial, political, and climatic conditions. As a result, more complex and faster supply chains will be forced to deal with increased uncertainty and volatility in both supply and demand. Finally, it must be noted, ongoing cost controls will mean that supply chain executives must deal with complexity, speed, and volatility with fewer resources—doing more with less. Being lean and mean, but in a more complex and volatile world, will be the great challenge of the future.

If the past is any guide, these topics will be addressed independently, and management guidelines, often put forth in two-by-two matrices, will be developed for each area of concern. The problem, of course, is that these issues are often inextricably interwoven, and actions taken to correct a problem in one area may very well initiate problems in another area. For example, the quest for fast and lean typically leads to a supply chain system with minimal inventories, rapid replenishment, and quick responses to shifts in demand patterns. In an era of heightened volatility, very fast responses to what may be noise rather than a sustained pattern can well introduce instability into the system. In other words, a system designed predominantly for speed and leanness may be ill suited to a period of great uncertainty. Understanding these interactions and their implications over time, and developing robust solutions, is the realm of system dynamics. Not only does each focus area have attributes that demand both a system and a dynamic perspective, but the overall system of issues must be addressed in an integrated fashion. Each trend and development must be understood on its own, but an integrated vision is also a must.

In Chapter 1, a simple one-stage model was used to demonstrate how system behavior is determined by structure, feedback, and delays. To illustrate the implications of complexity, consider the simple two-stage model shown in Figure 7.1. This model is a straightforward extension of the model in Chapter 1. The model in Chapter 1 considered only the retail sector and assumed that inventory was always available for shipment at the distributor and would arrive at the retailer after a processing and shipping delay. The two-stage model in Figure 7.1 replicates the basic inventory and ordering structure for the distributor and now includes orders being processed at the distributor, distributor desired inventory, distributor inventory, and orders to the factory by the distributor. It is assumed in this two-stage model that the factory has unlimited inventory and that shipments arrive at the distributor on average 5 weeks after the distributor places an order.

This model has been quantified to examine two modes of operation. One mode is deemed *moderate response* in that the delays, desired inventory coverage, and inventory correction factor are all in a slow to moderate range. The second mode is deemed *fast response* because of shortened delays, reduced desired inventory, and a higher inventory correction factor. The second mode is the more "lean and mean" response. It is assumed that in both modes, the distributor receives orders on average 5 weeks after placing the order with the factory. Figure 7.2 presents the values for the model parameters for both the retail and distributor stages of the model.

As in Chapter 1, a simulation is performed assuming that customer orders make a step increase of 20%, going from 10 per week to 12 per week at the end of week 4. Figure 7.3 presents the key rates for the moderate

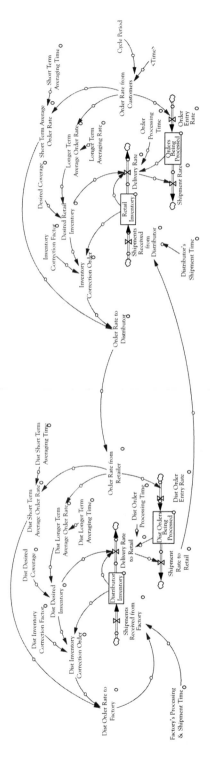

Figure 7.1. Two-stage model: Retail and distributor.

	Retail				
	Order Processing Time	Longer Term Averaging For Forecast	Shorter Term Averaging For Orders	Desired Inventory Coverage	Inventory Correction Factor
Moderate Response	0.5	4	2	2	0.25
Fast Response	0.2	2	1	1	0.5

	Distributor						Factory
	Order Processing Time	Longer Term Averaging For Forecast	Shorter Term Averaging For Orders	Desired Inventory Coverage	Inventory Correction Factor	Shipping Time To Retailer	Processing Shipping Time to Distributor
Moderate Response	0.5	4	2	2	1/4	1	5
Fast Response	0.2	2	1	1	1/2	0.5	5

Figure 7.2. Key model parameters for medium-response and fast-response two-stage system.

response system. In this case, the order rate to the distributor is very similar to that shown in Figure 1.6, but notice in Figure 7.3 the amplification that is present in the distributor's order rate to the factory. This amplification is a key danger arising with complexity. The amplification occurs because the distributor, with lack of point-of-sale data, is assuming the order rate from retail is a true indicator of consumer demand. In truth, retailer orders contain inventory-correction components as well. The distributor responds to these orders and then adds inventory-correcting terms to the basic order rate. As tiers are added in the supply chain, the risk grows for larger and larger swings for each succeeding lower-tier supplier. These broad swings in orders, for example, are often seen at the very end of supply chains in

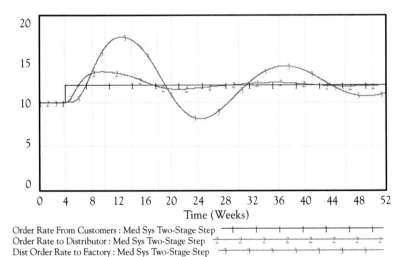

Order Rate From Customers : Med Sys Two-Stage Step
Order Rate to Distributor : Med Sys Two-Stage Step
Dist Order Rate to Factory : Med Sys Two-Stage Step

Figure 7.3. Key rates for medium-response two-stage system.

orders for commodities and for capital equipment. With greater complexity comes the strong need for visibility throughout the supply chain and for coordination and collaboration between tiers.

The goal of lean and mean supply chains brings additional risk on top of the complexity. Figure 7.4 presents the key rates for the fast response system, assuming the same 20% increase in customer orders at the end of week 4. Notice for this case an even greater amplification in the distributor's order rate to the factory. The moderate-response system showed overshoot and undershoot but, after a year, the order rate to the factory was settling down toward a steady state. For the fast-response system, however, severe oscillations continue with even a hint of instability. Even more telling is the behavior of inventories shown in Figure 7.5. This type of "boom or bust" cycling has been observed in numerous supply chains. With minimal inventories, the need for rapid correction is important but also threatening to stability. The challenge is that if one is "living inside" this type of supply chain behavior, it is difficult to diagnose the underlying phenomena from the symptoms. Much of this type of system behavior is self-imposed but in a way that makes it almost impossible to understand or correct. This is one of the great advantages of a system dynamics model—it facilitates understanding of system behavior and formulating corrective strategies.

In addition to complexity and speed, the main future challenge for supply chain executives will be dealing with increased volatility in economic and financial conditions. One approach to examining this issue of

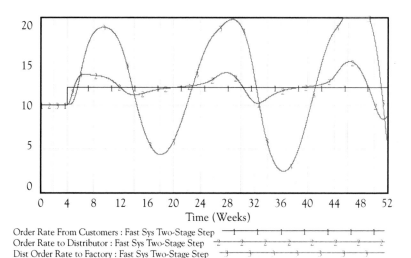

Order Rate From Customers : Fast Sys Two-Stage Step
Order Rate to Distributor : Fast Sys Two-Stage Step
Dist Order Rate to Factory : Fast Sys Two-Stage Step

Figure 7.4. Key rates for fast-response two-stage system.

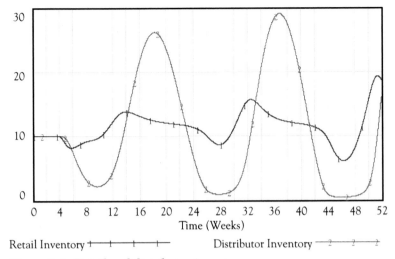

Retail Inventory ┼───┼───┼───┼───   Distributor Inventory ──2───2───2─

Figure 7.5. Retail and distributor inventory.

volatility is to assume cyclical or oscillating customer orders for both the moderate-response system and the fast-response system. This approach can illuminate the impacts of volatility on different systems and the system features that create greater susceptibility to volatility. Three rates of volatility are addressed: slow oscillation with a period of 1 year; moderate oscillation with a period of half a year (26 weeks); and fast oscillation with a period of a quarter of a year (13 weeks). Figure 7.6 illustrates these three patterns for order rates from customers.

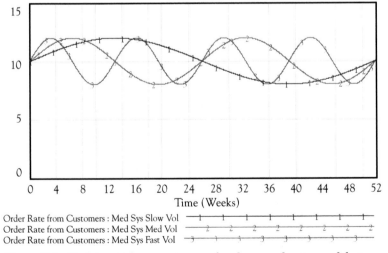

Order Rate from Customers : Med Sys Slow Vol   ─┼───┼───┼───┼───┼───┼───┼───┼─
Order Rate from Customers : Med Sys Med Vol   ──2───2───2───2───2───2───2───2─
Order Rate from Customers : Med Sys Fast Vol   ─3───3───3───3───3───3───3───3─

Figure 7.6. Order rate from customers for slow, moderate, and fast volatility.

Figures 7.7, 7.8, and 7.9 show simulation results for the order rate to the distributor, the distributor's order rate to the factory, and retail inventory for the moderate-response system for the three levels of volatility. It is somewhat surprising that all of these system variables show the greatest variability for the moderate level of volatility. Figures 7.10, 7.11, and 7.12 present the simulation results for the order rate to the distributor, the distributor's order rate to the factory, and retail inventory for the fast-response system for the three levels of volatility. Again it is notable that the variability in system behavior is greatest for the moderate level of volatility. One might intuitively surmise that the moderate-response system would show less variability for the moderate-volatility input and

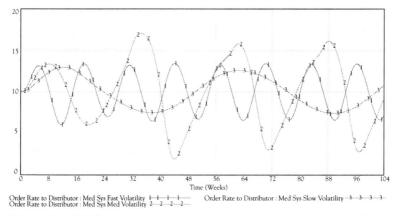

Figure 7.7. Moderate-response system: Order rate to distributor for slow, moderate, and fast volatility.

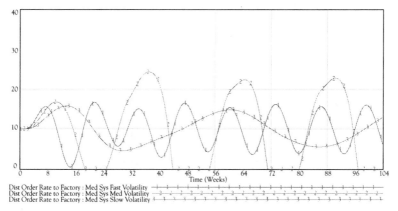

Figure 7.8. Moderate-response system: Order rate to factory for slow, moderate, and fast volatility.

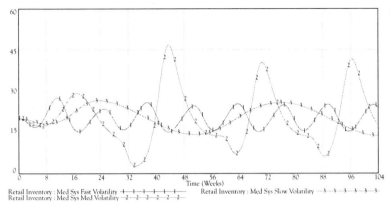

Figure 7.9. Moderate-response system: Retail inventory for slow, moderate, and fast volatility.

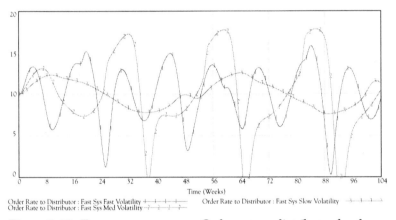

Figure 7.10. Fast-response system: Order rate to distributor for slow, moderate, and fast volatility.

that the fast-response system would show less variability for the fast oscillation. Both systems, however, exhibit greatest variability for not the slowest or the fastest but the moderate level of volatility. One of the great advantages of system dynamics is the ability to examine the causes of such nonintuitive behavior and the key factors driving such variability.

One key assumption for both the moderate-response system and the fast-response system in the aforementioned simulations is the 5-week processing and shipment time for factory orders. This is an approximation of typical shipping times from Asia to the United States. What if, for example, a factory warehouse might be established such that this

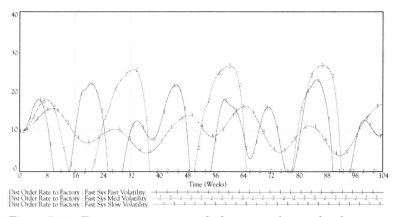

Figure 7.11. *Fast-response system: Order rate to factory for slow, moderate, and fast volatility.*

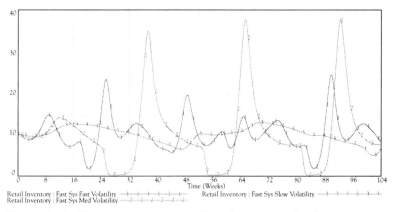

Figure 7.12. *Fast-response system: Retail inventory for slow, moderate, and fast volatility.*

delay was much shorter? How would faster service, although more costly, impact the wide swings in orders and inventories? Figures 7.13, 7.14, and 7.15 present simulation results for the moderate-response system with the system being driven by the midlevel volatility. In these cases, however, alternative times are assumed for the factory processing and shipping time. In the prior simulations, the factory processing and shipping time was assumed to be 5 weeks. In the following simulations, this 5-week assumption is referred to as the "slow factory" case. In the alternative assumptions, this factory response time is assumed to be 3 weeks for "medium factory" and one week for "fast factory."

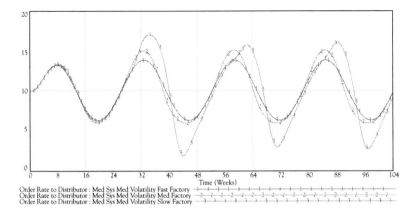

Figure 7.13. Moderate-response system and moderate volatility: Order rate to distributor with slow, medium, and fast factory times

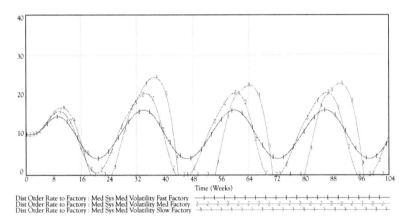

Figure 7.14. Moderate-response system and moderate volatility: Order rate to factory with slow, medium, and fast factory times.

As may be seen in these three charts, the variability for the order rates and inventory is dramatically stabilized for faster factory response times. Figures 7.16, 7.17, and 7.18 present simulation results for the fast-response system with factory processing and shipping times of 1, 3, and 5 weeks. Again, all of these simulations are being driven by the moderate level of oscillation, the condition creating the greatest variability in the system rates and inventories. And again, as for the moderate-response system, the variability is greatly stabilized by having the factory become more responsive.

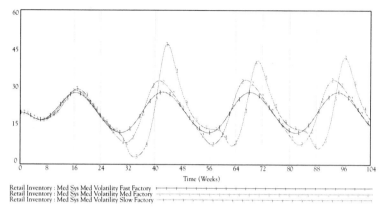

Figure 7.15. Moderate-response system and moderate volatility: Retail inventory with slow, medium, and fast factory times.

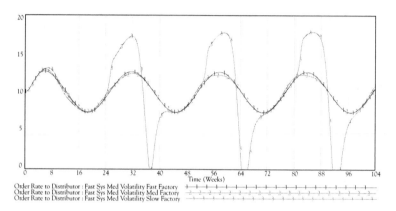

Figure 7.16. Fast-response system and moderate volatility: Order rate to distributor with slow, medium, and fast factory times.

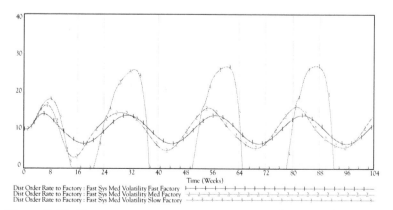

Figure 7.17. Fast-response system and moderate volatility: Distributor order rate to factory with slow, medium, and fast factory times.

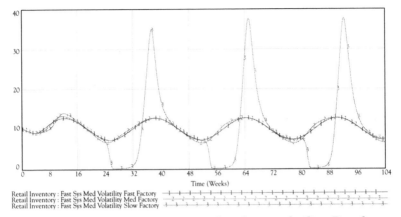

Figure 7.18. Fast-response system and moderate volatility: Retail inventory with slow, medium, and fast factory times.

As supply chains, now more accurately described as *highly distributed supply networks*, become ever more complex and subject to heightened volatility and uncertainty, the role and contributions of system dynamics will only increase. System dynamics models will provide the foundation for stabilizing system behavior. Moreover, because of inevitable disruptions and volatility, the network will occasionally be disturbed from its prescribed operational mode. In those cases, system dynamics will provide the analytical tools for planning recovery in a timely but stabilizing fashion.

Notes

Introduction

1. Simchi-Levi, Kaminsky, and Simchi-Levi (2008).
2. "Bullwhip" Hits Firms as Growth Snaps Back (January 27, 2010).

Chapter 1

1. Forrester (1961); Sterman (2000).

Chapter 2

1. Rosenman and Hoekstra (1964).
2. Rosenman (1980).
3. Rosenman (1981).
4. Government Accountability Office (GAO, 1981).
5. GAO (1990).
6. GAO (1998).
7. GAO (2007a).
8. GAO (2007b).
9. Thorne (1999).
10. Forrester (1958).
11. Forrester (1961).
12. Sterman (2000).
13. Huang and Wang (2007); Sterman (2000).
14. Schroeter and Spengler (2005).
15. Simchi-Levi, Kaminsky, and Simchi-Levi (2008); Lee, Padmanabhan, and Whang (1997).
16. Angerhofer and Angelides (2000).
17. Sterman (2000).
18. GAO (1981); GAO (2007b).
19. Ott and Longnecker (2010).
20. Rosenman (1981).

Chapter 3

1. Avery (2007).
2. Abramson and Harris (2003); Folkeson and Brauner (2005); Gansler and Luby (2003).
3. Rosenman and Hoekstra (1964).
4. Killingsworth, Chavez, and Martin (2008a).
5. Killingsworth, Chavez, and Martin (2008b).
6. Government Accountability Office (GAO, 1981); GAO (2007c).
7. Forrester (1961).

Chapter 4

1. Simchi-Levi, Kaminski, and Simchi-Levi (2004); Nahmias (1997).
2. Macy (1945).
3. Thorne (1999).
4. Abramson and Harris (2003); Folkeson and Brauner (2005); Gansler and Luby (2004).
5. Rosenman and Hoekstra (1964).
6. Malehorn (2001).
7. Safavi (2005).
8. Killingsworth, Chavez, and Martin (2008a).
9. Folkeson and Brauner (2005).
10. Case study (2004).
11. Simchi-Levi, Kaminski, and Simchi-Levi (2008).
12. Supply chain optimization (1999).
13. Government Accountability Office (GAO, 2007).
14. Folkeson and Brauner (2005).
15. Simchi-Levi et al. (2008).
16. Villa and Watanabe (1993).
17. Minnich and Maier (2007).
18. Folkeson and Brauner (2005).
19. Chandra and Grabis (2006).
20. Lan, Chu, Chung, Wan, and Lo (1999).
21. Simchi-Levi and Zhao (2005).
22. Lee, Chew, Teng, and Chen (2008).
23. Killingsworth, Chavez, and Martin (2008b).
24. Killingsworth, Chavez, and Martin (2008c).
25. Thorne (1999).

Chapter 5

1. Ain (2009); Anthony (2009); Gottlieb (2008); Shute (2009).
2. United States Department of Defense (1995).
3. Government Accountability Office (GAO, 2003).
4. United States Department of Defense (2009).
5. Forbes, Hees, Long, and Stouffer (2007).
6. Forbes et al. (2007).
7. Rosenman and Hoekstra (1964).
8. Killingsworth, Chavez, and Martin (2008).

Chapter 6

1. Government Accountability Office (GAO, 2003).
2. Forbes, Hees, Long, and Stouffer (2007); McQueary (2009).
3. Killingsworth, Speciale, and Martin (2009).
4. Killingsworth, Chavez, and Martin (2008).
5. Rosenman and Hoekstra (1964).
6. Killingsworth, Speciale, and Martin (2009).

References

Aerospace Industries Association. Life cycle sustainment: Accomplishing performance driven outcomes through condition based maintenance and continuous process improvement. Retrieved from http://www.aia-aerospace.org/assets/wp_pdo-cbm.pdf.

Ain, A. (2009, April 22). Doing more with less. *Business Week.*

Angerhofer, B. J., & Angelides, M. C. (2000, December). System dynamics modelling in supply chain management: Research review. Paper presented at 2000 Winter Simulation Conference, Orlando, FL.

Anthony, S. (2009, February 26). Creative innovation: Doing more with less. *Forbes.*

Avery, S. (2007, October). Boeing executive Steven Schaffer is named supply chain manager of the year for the 787 Dreamliner project. *Purchasing.*

"Bullwhip" hits firms as growth snaps back. (2010, January 27). *Wall Street Journal.*

Case study: Air Force materiel command hikes availability. (2004, May), *Purchasing*, 133(9).

Chandra, C., & Grabis, J. (2006). Inventory management with variable lead-time dependent procurement cost. *Omega, 36(5), 877– 887.*

Correa, E. (2007, October 31). Aviation engineering reliability and sustainment programs. Defense Logistics Agency. Defense Supply Center Richmond. Retrieved from http://www.acq.osd.mil/log/mpp/cbm+/DSCR_aviation_engin_Oct07_2.ppt.

Folkeson, J. R., & Brauner, M. K. (2005). Improving the Army's management of reparable spare parts. Santa Monica, CA: RAND.

Forbes, J., Hees, J., Long, A. E., & Stouffer, V. (2007, June). Empirical relationships between reliability investments and life-cycle support costs. LMI Government Consulting. Report SA701TI.

Forrester, J. W. (1958, July–August). Industrial dynamics: A major breakthrough for decision makers. *Harvard Business Review.*

Forrester, J. W. (1961). *Industrial dynamics.* Cambridge, MA: MIT Press.

Gansler, J. S., & Luby, R. E. Jr. (2004). *Transforming government supply chain management.* New York: Rowman and Littlefield.

Gottlieb, H. (2008, December 9). Doing more with less in hard times. *Chronicle of Philanthropy.*

Government Accountability Office. (1981, December 1). The army should improve its requirements determination system (PLRD-82-19).

Government Accountability Office. (1990, September 11). Army inventory: Army annually spends millions to keep retention-level stocks (NSIAD-90-236).

Government Accountability Office. (1998, February). Inventory management: DOD can build on progress by using best practices for reparable parts (GAO-NSIAD-98-97).

Government Accountability Office. (2001, July). Army inventory: Parts shortages are impacting operations and maintenance effectiveness (GAO-01-772).

Government Accountability Office. (2003, February). Setting requirements differently could reduce weapon systems' total ownership costs (GAO-03-57).

Government Accountability Office. (2007a, January). DOD's high-risk areas: Progress made implementing supply chain management recommendations, but full extent of improvement unknown (GAO-07-234).

Government Accountability Office. (2007b, March 2). Defense inventory: Opportunities exist to improve the management of DOD's acquisition lead times for spare parts (GAO-07-281).

Government Accountability Office. (2007c, July 10). DOD's high-risk areas: Efforts to improve supply chain can be enhanced by linkage to outcomes, progress in transforming business operations, and reexamination of logistics governance and strategy (GAO-07-1064T).

Government Accountability Office. (2008, December). Defense logistics: Improved analysis and cost data needed to evaluate the cost-effectiveness of performance based logistics (GAO-09-41).

http://www.purchasing.com/article/CA6489135.html?q=Distributor+technology +can+remove+costs+from+the+supply+chain+&q=boeing+supplier+collaboration (accessed March 26, 2008).

Huang, L., & Wang, Q. (2007, July 29–August 2). The bullwhip effect in the closed loop supply chain. Paper presented at 2007 International Conference of the System Dynamics Society and 50th Anniversary Celebration, Boston, MA.

Killingsworth, W. R., Chavez, R. K., & Martin, N. T. (2008a, July 20–24).The dynamics of multi-tier, multi-channel supply chains for high-value government aviation parts. Paper accepted for presentation at 26th International Conference of the System Dynamics Society, Athens, Greece.

Killingsworth, W. R., Chavez, R. K., & Martin, N. T. (2008b, July 20–24). The dynamics of the government supply process for high-value spare parts. Paper submitted to 26th International Conference of the System Dynamics Society, Athens, Greece.

Killingsworth, W. R., Chavez, R. K., & Martin, N. T. (2008c, July 20–24). The dynamics of multi-channel supply chains for high-value government aviation parts. Paper submitted to 26th International Conference of the System Dynamics Society, Athens, Greece.

Killingsworth, W. R., Speciale, S. M., & Martin, N. T. (2010, July 25–29). Achieving reductions in life-cycle costs through investments in improved reliability. Paper submitted to 28th International Conference of the System Dynamics Society, Seoul, Korea.

Kim, S.-H., Cohen, M. A., & Netessine, S. (2009, September 10). Reliability or inventory? Analysis of product support contracts in the defense industry. Retrieved from http://www.som.yale.edu/faculty/sangkim/ReliabilityInventory.pdf.

Lan, S.-P., Chu, P., Chung, K.-J., Wan, W.-J., & Lo, R. (1999). A simple method to locate the optimal solution of the inventory model with variable lead time. *Computers & Operations Research, 26(6)*, 599–605.

Lee, H. L., Padmanabhan, V., & Whang, S. (1997). The bullwhip effect in supply chains. *Sloan Management Review, 3837*(Spring), 93–102.

Lee, L. H., Chew, E. P., Teng, S., & Chen, Y. (2008). Multi-objective simulation-based evolutionary algorithm for an aircraft spare parts allocation problem. *European Journal of Operational Research, 189*(2), 476–491.

Macy, R. M. (1945, October). Forecasting demand for U.S. Army supplies in wartime. *Journal of Marketing.*

Malehorn, J. (2001). Forecasting at Lockheed Martin Aircraft and Logistics Centers. *Journal of business forecasting methods & systems, 20*(3).

McQueary, C. E. (2009, January 15). Life cycle costs savings by improving reliability. Operational Test and Evaluation, Office of the Secretary of Defense.

Minnich, D., & Maier, F. (2006, July 23–27). Supply chain responsiveness and efficiency—Complementing or contradicting each other? Paper presented at 2006 International Conference of the System Dynamics Society, Nijmegen, Netherlands.

Minnich, D., & Maier, F. (2007, July 29–August 2). Responsiveness and efficiency of pull-based and push-based planning systems in the high-tech electronics industry. Paper presented at 2007 International Conference of the System Dynamics Society and 50th Anniversary Celebration, Boston, MA.

Nahmias, S. (1997). *Production and operations analysis* (3rd ed.). New York: McGraw-Hill Irwin.

Ott, R. L., & Longnecker, M. (2010). *An introduction to statistical methods and data analysis* (6th ed.). Belmont, CA: Brooks/Cole.

Paulraj, A., & Chen, I. J. (2007). Environmental uncertainty and strategic supply management: A resource dependence perspective and performance implications. *Journal of Supply Chain Management, 43*(3).

Rosenman, B. B. (1980, November). CCSS supply management. *IRO* Report No. 280.

Rosenman, B. B. (1981, June). Supply control study instability. *IRO* Report No. 285.

Rosenman, B., & Hoekstra, D. (1964, October). A management system for high-value army aviation components. *IRO* Report No. TR-64-1.

Safavi, A. (2005). Forecasting demand in the aerospace and defense industry. *Journal of Business Forecasting, 24*(1).

Schroeter, M., & Spengler, T. (2005, July 17–21). A system dynamics model for strategic management of spare parts in closed-loop supply chains. Paper presented at 23rd International Conference of the System Dynamics Society, Boston, MA.

Shute, T. (2009, August 5). Energy companies doing more with less. *Motley Fool.*

Simchi-Levi, D., Kaminsky, P., & Simchi-Levi, E. (2004) *Managing the supply chain.* New York: McGraw-Hill.

Simchi-Levi, D., Kaminsky, P., & Simchi-Levi, E. (2008). *Designing and managing the supply chain: Concepts, strategies and case studies.* New York: McGraw-Hill Irwin.

Simchi-Levi, D., & Zhao, Y. (2005). Safety stock positioning in supply chains with stochastic lead times. *Manufacturing and service operations management, 7*(4), 295–318.

Sterman, J. D. (2000). Business dynamics: Systems thinking and modeling for a complex world. New York: McGraw-Hill.

Teresko, J. (2007, December). The Boeing 787: A matter of materials. *Industry Week.*

Thorne, S. C. (1999). *Rightsizing DOD inventory: A critical look at excesses, incentives and cultural change* (Master's thesis, Naval Postgraduate School). Retrieved from http://edocs.nps.edu/npspubs/scholarly/theses/1999/Dec/99Dec_Thorne.pdf.

United States Department of Defense. (2009, June 1). *Reliability, availability, maintainability, and cost rationale report manual.* Presented by the Office of the Secretary of Defense in Collaboration with the Joint Staff.

United States Department of Defense. (1995, February 13). *DoD News Briefing: Dr. Paul Kaminski.* Presented by Dr. Paul Kaminski. Retrieved from http://www.defense.gov/Transcripts/Transcript.aspx?TranscriptID=102.

Villa, A., & Watanabe, T. (1993). Production management: Beyond the dichotomy between "push" and "pull." *Computer Integrated Manufacturing Systems, 6*(1), 53–63.

Index

Note: The italicized *t* and *f* following page numbers refer to tables and figures.

Announcing the Business Expert Press Digital Library

Concise E-books Business Students Need for Classroom and Research

This book can also be purchased in an e-book collection by your library as

- a one-time purchase,
- that is owned forever,
- allows for simultaneous readers,
- has no restrictions on printing, and
- can be downloaded as PDFs from within the library community.

Our digital library collections are a great solution to beat the rising cost of textbooks. E-books can be loaded into their course management systems or onto student's e-book readers.

The **Business Expert Press** digital libraries are very affordable, with no obligation to buy in future years.

For more information, please visit **www.businessexpert.com/libraries**. To set up a trial in the United States, please contact **Sheri Allen** at *sheri.allen@globalepress.com*; for all other regions, contact **Nicole Lee** at *nicole.lee@igroupnet.com*.

CPSIA information can be obtained at www.ICGtesting.com

264301BV00005B/6/P